Balconville

BALCONVILLE

a play by David Fennario

Talonbooks
P.O. Box 2076, Vancouver, British Columbia, Canada V6B 3S3
www.talonbooks.com

Printed and bound in Canada by Hignell Book Printing.

Published with the assistance of the Canada Council.

Sixth Printing: January 2001

Canadian Cataloguing in Publication Data

Fennario, David, 1947–
  Balconville

  ISBN 0-88922-145-6

  I. Title.
PS 8561.E54B34   C812 .54   C81-091041-1
PR9199.3.F45B34

Balconville was commissioned by and first performed at Centaur Theatre in Montréal, Québec on January 2, 1979, with the following cast:

Thibault	Jean Archambault
Diane Paquette	Manon Bourgeois
Irene Regan	Lynne Deragon
Claude Paquette	Marc Gelinas
Johnny Regan	Peter MacNeill
Tom Williams	Robert Parson
Cécile Paquette	Cécile St-Denis
Muriel Williams	Terry Tweed

Directed by Guy Sprung
Designed by Barbra Matis
Lighting by Steven Hawkins

Balconville was also performed at the St. Lawrence Centre in Toronto, Ontario on October 3, 1979 and at the National Art Centre in Ottawa, Ontario on November 5, 1979, with the following cast:

Thibault	Jean Archambault
Diane Paquette	Manon Bourgeois
Irene Regan	Anne Anglin
Claude Paquette	Marc Gelinas
Johnny Regan	Peter MacNeill
Tom Williams	Robert Parson
Cécile Paquette	Yolande Circé
Muriel Williams	Terry Tweed
Gaëtan Bolduc	Gilles Tordjman

Directed by Guy Sprung
Designed by Barbra Matis
Lighting by Steven Hawkins

Act One
Scene One

It is night. TOM is sitting on his back balcony trying to play "Mona" on his guitar. The sound of a car screeching around a corner is heard. The car beeps its horn. DIANE enters.

VOICE: Diane, Diane . . .

DIANE: J'savais que t'avais une autre blonde.

VOICE: Mais non, Diane, c'était ma soeur.

DIANE: Oui, ta soeur. Mange d'la merde. Fuck you!

CECILE comes out of her house and stands on her balcony.

CECILE: C'est-tu, Jean-Guy? Diane?

DIANE: Oh, achale-moi pas.

The car screeches away.

MURIEL: *from the screen door behind TOM*
    Goddamn teenagers, they don't stop until they kill someone. Tommy, what are you doing there?

The sound of the car screeching is heard on the other side of the stage.

VOICE: Hey, Diane. Diane. . .

DIANE: Maudit crisse, va-t'en, hostie.

CECILE: Diane, c'est Jean-Guy.

VOICE: Hey, Diane. Viens-t'en faire un tour avec moi, Diane?

The car beeps its horn.

DIANE: Jamais, jamais. J't'haïs, j't'haïs.

VOICE: Hey, Diane.

The car beeps its horn again.

PAQUETTE: *from inside his house*   Qu'est-ce qu'y a? Qu'est-ce tu veux, hostie?

VOICE: Diane, viens ici.

PAQUETTE: *yelling from the upstairs window*   Si tu t'en vas pas, j'appelle la police.

Muriel comes out of her house, goes down the alley and yells after the car.

MURIEL: Get the hell out of here, you goddamn little creep!

The car screeches away. MURIEL returns to her house.

MURIEL: *to TOM*   Tom you gotta get up tomorrow.

TOM: Yeah, yeah.

MURIEL goes into her house.

PAQUETTE: Maudit crisse, j'te dis que t'en as des amis toi. C'est la dernière fois que je te préviens. Cécile, viens-tu t'coucher?

CECILE: Oui, oui, Claude, j'arrive. Diane, Jean-Guy devrait pas venir si tard.

DIANE: Ah, parle-moi pu d'lui.

CECILE: Son char fait bien trop de train, y devrait faire réparer son muffler.

CECILE goes into her house with DIANE.

JOHNNY enters. He is drunk and singing "Heartbreak Hotel." He finds that the door to his house is locked.

JOHNNY: Hey, Irene. . . . Irene, open the fuckin' door.

IRENE opens the door.

PAQUETTE: *from inside his house*   Hey! Ferme ta gueule, toi-là.

JOHNNY: Fuck you!

He goes into his house and slams the door shut.

Blackout.

Scene Two

The next day. It is morning. THIBAULT enters wheeling his Chez Momo's delivery bike down the lane. TOM comes out of the house with toast, coffee, cigarettes and his guitar. When he is finished his toast and coffee, he begins to practise his guitar.

MURIEL: *from inside her house* Tom, you left the goddamn toaster on again.

TOM: Yeah?

MURIEL: Yeah, well, I'm the one who pays the electric bills.

THIBAULT looks at the tire on his delivery bike.

THIBAULT: Câlice, how did that happen? The tire, c'est fini.

TOM: A flat.

THIBAULT: Eh?

TOM: A flat tire.

THIBAULT: Ben oui, un flat tire. The other one, she's okay. . . . That's funny, eh? Very funny, that.

TOM: Don't worry, Thibault, it's only flat on the bottom.

THIBAULT: You think so? Well, I got to phone the boss.

He goes up the stairs and steps over the broken step.

TOM: Hey, watch the step!

THIBAULT: *knocking on PAQUETTE's door* Paquette, Paquette. . . .

PAQUETTE: *from inside his house*   Tabarnac, c'est quoi?

THIBAULT: C'est moi, Paquette. J'ai un flat tire.

PAQUETTE: Cécile, la porte. . . .

CECILE: *from inside the house*   Oui, oui. . . . Une minute. . . .

THIBAULT: C'est moi, Paquette.

CECILE: *at the screen door*   Allô, Thibault. Comment ça va?

THIBAULT: J'ai un flat tire sur mon bicycle.

CECILE: Oh, un flat tire.

PAQUETTE: Que c'est qu'y a?

CECILE: C'est Thibault, Claude.

PAQUETTE: Thibault? Thibault?

THIBAULT: Oui. Bonjour.

PAQUETTE: Es-tu tombé sur la tête, tabarnac? Il est sept heures et demie du matin, hostie de ciboire.

CECILE: Claude a travaillé tard hier soir.

THIBAULT: That's not so good, eh?

PAQUETTE: Que c'est qu'y veut?

CECILE: Y veux savoir c'que tu veux.

THIBAULT: *yelling at PAQUETTE through the window*
J'ai un flat tire. Je voudrais téléphoner à mon boss.

PAQUETTE: Crie pas si fort, j'suis pas sourd. Cécile, dis-lui de rentrer.

JOHNNY: *from inside his house*   What the fuck's going on?

THIBAULT: C'est-tu, okay?

CECILE: Oui, oui. Entre.

THIBAULT goes into PAQUETTE's house. JOHNNY comes out on his balcony.

JOHNNY: What's going on?

TOM: *from below*   Thibault's got a flat tire.

JOHNNY: Flat tire? Big fuckin' production!

He goes back into his house

THIBAULT: *inside PAQUETTE's house*   Allô, Paquette. J'vas téléphoner à mon boss. C'est-tu, okay? C'est-tu, okay?

PAQUETTE: *from inside his house*   Ferme ta gueule! Tu m'as réveillé asteur. Fais ce que t'as à faire.

THIBAULT: *on the telephone*   Oui, allô, Monsieur Kryshinsky. . . . This is the right number? This is Monsieur Krychinsky? . . . Bon. C'est moi, Thibault. . . . Oui. . . . Quoi? . . . Yes, I'm not there. I'm here. . . .

CECILE: *from inside the house*   Veux-tu ton déjeuner, Claude?

PAQUETTE: Non, fais-moi un café. Ça va faire.

THIBAULT: Un flat tire, oui. . . . Okay. Yes, sir. I'll be there. . . . Oui. I'll be there tout de suite. . . . Okay, boss. Bye. . . . Allô? Bye.

12

He hangs up the telephone.

THIBAULT: Faut que j'm'en aille. C'était mon boss. Tu
le connais, "I don't like it when you're late. When I get to
the store, I want you there at the door. Right there at the
door."

PAQUETTE pushes THIBAULT outside.

PAQUETTE: *standing at the door*   Salut, Thibault.
Salut, Thibault.

THIBAULT: Okay, salut.

*Coming down the stairs, THIBAULT trips on the broken
step and loses his cap.*

TOM: *from below*   Watch the step!

THIBAULT: Hey, that was a close one. Very close, that
one.

THIBAULT exits on his bike.

PAQUETTE: *on his balcony*   Cécile, est-ce que
Diane veut un lift pour aller à l'école?

CECILE: *at the screen door*   Diane?

DIANE: *from inside the house*   Non.

PAQUETTE: Pourquoi faire?

DIANE: Parce que j'aime pas la manière qu'y chauffe son
char.

CECILE: Elle a dit que. . . .

PAQUETTE: J'suis pas sourd. Qu'elle s'arrange pas pour
manquer ses cours, c'est moi qui les paye cet été.

DIANE: Inquiète-toi pas avec ça.

JOHNNY comes out on his balcony again.

PAQUETTE: *to JOHNNY*   Hey, people gotta sleep at night, eh?

JOHNNY: You talking to me?

PAQUETTE: *pointing to the wall*   No, him. Hostie.

CECILE: Claude, j'pense que ce soir, je vais te faire des bonnes tourtières. Tu sais celles que t'aimes, celles du Lac St-Jean.

PAQUETTE: Encore des tourtières?

CECILE: Claude, t'aimes ça des tourtières.

PAQUETTE: Oui, j'aime ça des tourtières, mais pas tous les jours.

DIANE: *from inside the house*   Maman, où sont mes souliers . . . mes talons hauts?

CECILE: J'sais pas. Où est-ce que tu les as mis hier soir?

She disappears into the house.

PAQUETTE: Cécile, j'm'en vas.

JOHNNY: Watch the step!

PAQUETTE: *coming down the stairs*   C'est qui qui a encore laissé les vidanges en dessous des escaliers?

TOM: *from below*   Not me.

PAQUETTE: It's me who got the trouble with the landlord, eh?

CECILE comes running out on the balcony with PAQUETTE's lunchbucket.

CECILE: Claude, Claude. . . . T'as oublié ton lunch.

PAQUETTE: C'est l'affaire de Thibault. . . . Pitch-moi-la.

CECILE tosses him his lunch.

JOHNNY: Baloney sandwiches again, eh, Porky?

PAQUETTE exits. IRENE comes out on her balcony to take the underwear off the clothesline.

JOHNNY: What time is it, Irene?

IRENE: *looking at him* You look a wreck.

JOHNNY: You don't look so hot yourself.

IRENE: You're beginning to look like a boozer, ya know that?

JOHNNY: Hey, all I want is the time.

DIANE comes out on the balcony carrying her school books.

DIANE: J'perds mon temps avec ce maudit cours stupide, surtout l'été.

CECILE: Diane, est-ce que tu vas venir souper?

DIANE: Peut-être.

CECILE goes back into her house. DIANE comes down the stairs. She is wearing shorts and high heels. JOHNNY and TOM both look at her.

JOHNNY: Hey, Diane, ya look like a flamingo in those things.

DIANE makes a face at him and exits down the lane.

IRENE: You like that, eh?

JOHNNY: Just looking.

IRENE: Well, no more meat and potatoes for you.

JOHNNY: Eh?

IRENE: You know what I mean.

JOHNNY: What?

IRENE goes back into the house.

JOHNNY: Fuck!

TOM: She's mad, eh?

JOHNNY: Ya ask her for the time and she tells ya how to make a watch.

He listens to TOM practicing his guitar.

JOHNNY: Hey, softer on the strings. Strum them, don't bang them.

TOM tries strumming.

TOM: Like that?

JOHNNY: Yeah, sort of . . . .

TOM: You used to play, eh?

JOHNNY: Yeah. Ever heard of "J.R. and the Falling Stars?"

TOM: No.

JOHNNY: You're looking at "J.R."

MURIEL comes out of her house carrying a bag of garbage.

MURIEL: *to TOM*   What are you doing?

TOM: The U.I.C. don't open till nine o'clock.

MURIEL: Yeah, but there's gonna be a line-up.

TOM: It's a waste of time. They never get ya jobs anyhow.

MURIEL: Well, don't think you're gonna hang around
    here doing nothing.

TOM: Okay, okay. Ma, I need some bus fare and some
    money for lunch.

MURIEL: You can come home for lunch.

TOM: Ma . . . .

MURIEL: I'm not giving you any money to bum around
    with.

TOM goes into the house with his guitar.

MURIEL: And you leave my purse alone in there too.

TOM comes back out with her purse.

TOM: Ma, I want my allowance.

MURIEL: What allowance? You don't go to school no
    more.

TOM: I want my money.

MURIEL: Gimme that purse. Gimme that goddamn
    purse.

She snatches her purse away from TOM, opens it and gives him some bus tickets.

MURIEL: That's it . . . . That's all you get.

TOM: Fuck!

MURIEL: Don't swear at me. Don't you ever swear at me.

TOM exits.

JOHNNY: *singing*   "Hi-ho, hi-ho, it's off to work we go."

MURIEL: *to JOHNNY*   You're not funny.

JOHNNY: You're a little hard on the kid, aren't ya, Muriel?

MURIEL: Yeah, well, look what happened to you.

JOHNNY: Fuck! What's with everybody today? Is it the heat or what?

He goes into his house. CECILE comes out on her balcony. She notices MURIEL's wash hanging from the clothesline.

CECILE: It's so nice to see that, madame.

MURIEL: See what?

CECILE: To see you put up the washing the right way. First the white clothes, then the dark ones. The young girls, they don't care anymore.

MURIEL: Yeah, well, why should they?

CECILE: Having children is not easy today? Eh?

MURIEL: Ah, they don't know what's good for them.

CECILE: Oui, I suppose.

MURIEL: When I was a kid, you just did what you were told and that was it.

CECILE: Yes, I remember that too.

MURIEL: Everybody got along alright. Now, nobody knows their ass from their elbow.

CECILE: Elbow?...Yes....

THIBAULT enters on his bike again. He is looking for his cap.

CECILE: Allô, Thibault. Comment ça va?

THIBAULT: Ma casquette. . . .

CECILE: Ta casquette?

THIBAULT: Ben oui, j'ai perdu ma casquette. Oh, elle est en bas.

He looks under the stairs and finds his cap.

THIBAULT: J'veux pas la perdre. J'ai payé quatre dollars chez Kresge.

CECILE: Eh, Thibault, ton boss était pas trop fâché?

THIBAULT: Il a sacré un peu après moi, but so what, eh? Il est jamais content anyway. Qu'tu fasses n'importe quoi.

CECILE: C'est la vie, hein ça?

THIBAULT: Oh, oui. C'est la vie.

He checks his transistor radio.

THIBAULT: Hey, thirty-two degrees. That used to be cold. Now, it's hot.

CECILE: Comment va ta mère? Est-ce qu'elle va toujours à Notre-Dame-des-Sept-Douleurs?

THIBAULT: Oh, oui. Tous les jours. Mes frères sont tous partis, mais moi, j'suis toujours avec.

CECILE: C'est bien ça. Ta mère doit être contente.

THIBAULT: J'fais toute pour elle. Toute. Dans un an, elle va recevoir sa old age pension et puis on va pouvoir s'payer un plus grand logement. On va déménager à Verdun.

CECILE: A Verdun. Ça va être bien ça. Thibault, ton boss.

THIBAULT: Oh, oui. Mon boss. I better go now.

THIBAULT exits. MURIEL's phone rings. She goes into her house to answer it. CECILE goes into her house.

MURIEL: *on the telephone* Yeah, hello....Who?... Bill, where the hell are ya?...On the docks...shipping out to Sault Ste-Marie....Are you coming back or what?...Don't give me that crap. What's her name, eh?...Yeah, I'm getting the cheques....Tom? No, he's not here....Yeah....Yeah....Look, I'm busy....Bye.

She hangs up the telephone.

MURIEL: Christ, I wish I knew for sure.

IRENE and JOHNNY come out on their balcony. JOHNNY is sipping a cup of coffee. IRENE is wearing her waitress uniform. She is on her way to work.

IRENE: I want to talk to you when I get back, Johnny.

JOHNNY: Yeah, yeah. Talk. *Sipping his coffee.* Agh! What are you trying to do, poison me?

IRENE: I used brown sugar instead of white.

JOHNNY: Shit.

IRENE: It's healthier for you. . . . You going down to the
     U.I.C.?

JOHNNY: Yeah.

IRENE: Today?

JOHNNY: Yeah, today.

IRENE starts to come down the stairs.

JOHNNY: Irene, what shift are you on?

IRENE: Ten to six this week.

JOHNNY: Why don't you quit that fucking job? Get
     something else.

IRENE: *stopping*   Like what?

JOHNNY: Like anything except a waitress.

IRENE continues down the stairs and exits down the lane.

JOHNNY: *shouting after her*   Pick me up a carton of
     smokes, I'm sick of these rollies.

Blackout.

Scene Three

TOM and JOHNNY enter from the alley. JOHNNY is carrying a case of beer.

JOHNNY: I'm telling ya, they're all fucking separatists at the U.I.C. If you're English, you're fucked.

TOM: The phones are always ringing and nobody ever answers them. Ever noticed that?

JOHNNY: Too busy having coffee breaks.

He hands TOM a beer.

JOHNNY: Unenjoyment disappointment office.

JOHNNY sits at the foot of the stairs. TOM leans on the railing.

TOM: Hey, I went down to Northern Electric. I figured I've been breathing in their smoke all my life, so the least they could do is give me a job. Didn't get one.... They're automating.

MURIEL comes out of her house.

JOHNNY: Hi, Muriel.

MURIEL: *to TOM*   What are you doing?

TOM: Standing up.

JOHNNY: Wanna brew, Muriel?

MURIEL: I told you to keep your goddamn beer to yourself. Tom, come here.

TOM: What?

MURIEL: Never mind what. Just come here.

TOM moves towards her.

MURIEL: So, did you go to that job interview?

TOM: Yeah.

MURIEL: So?

TOM: So, the guy didn't like me.

MURIEL: He didn't like you? How come?

TOM: I dunno.

MURIEL: What do you mean, you dunno?

TOM: He wanted to send me to some stupid joe job way
out in Park Extension. Minimum wage.

MURIEL: Since when can you afford to be fussy?

TOM: I'd have to get up at five in the morning.

MURIEL: There's a lot of things I don't like either, but I
do them.

TOM: Well, I don't.

MURIEL: Anyhow, your father phoned. He's not coming
home.

TOM: I don't blame him.

MURIEL: What's that?

TOM: Forget it.

MURIEL: Don't you get into one of your moods, mister,
'cause I'll give it to you right back.

MURIEL goes into her house.

TOM: Fuckin' bitch!

JOHNNY: Hey, don't worry about it.

TOM: Just 'cause she's frustrated, don't mean she's gotta take it out on me.

JOHNNY: Let them scream, that's what I do.

JOHNNY leaves TOM and starts up the stairs for his balcony. TOM goes into his house to get his guitar. CECILE comes out on her balcony with a handful of breadcrumbs. She starts to feed the birds.

CECILE: Hi, Johnny.

JOHNNY: Hi, Cécile.

CECILE: Nice day, eh?

JOHNNY: Yeah, but it's too hot.

CECILE: Oh yes, too hot.

She continues feeding the birds.

JOHNNY: Feeding your Air Force?

CECILE: My what?

JOHNNY: Your Air Force . . . . Cécile's Air Force.

CECILE: Ah, oui. Air Force.

JOHNNY: Just kidding ya, Cécile.

He sits on his balcony with his beer.

CECILE: You just kidding me, eh, Johnny?

She throws some more breadcrumbs over the railing. They fall on MURIEL as she comes out of her house carrying a basket of washing.

MURIEL: Jesus Murphy!

CECILE: Oh, excuse me, madame. Excuse me. Hello!

MURIEL: Yeah, hello. . . .

CECILE: Aw, it's so nice, eh?

MURIEL: What?

CECILE: The sun. It's so nice, eh?

MURIEL: What?

CECILE: The sun. It's so nice.

MURIEL: Yeah, I guess it is.

CECILE: It's so good for my plants.

JOHNNY: How are your tomatoes?

CECILE: My tomatoes? Very good. This year, I think I get some big ones. Last year, I don't know what happened to them.

JOHNNY: The cat pissed on them.

CECILE: The what?

JOHNNY: The big tomcat that's always hanging around with Muriel. He pissed on them.

CECILE: You think so?

JOHNNY: Sure.

CECILE sits on her balcony. TOM comes out of the house again and sits practicing his guitar.

JOHNNY: *to TOM*   Too heavy on the strings. . . .

PAQUETTE enters carrying his lunchbucket. He is coming home from work.

JOHNNY: Hey, the working man!

PAQUETTE: Somebody has to work, eh?

He starts to climb the stairs. JOHNNY stops him.

JOHNNY: Have a brew here.

PAQUETTE: Okay.

He takes a pint from JOHNNY and sits down on JOHNNY's balcony.

PAQUETTE: Hey, my car, it's not working again. That goddamn carburetor. . . .   *To CECILE, on her balcony.*   Cécile. . . . Hey, Cécile.

CECILE: Oui.

PAQUETTE: J'vas manger plus tard.

CECILE: Quoi?

PAQUETTE: *shouting at her*   J'vas manger plus tard.

CECILE: Tu vas manger plus tard?

PAQUETTE: Oui, tabarnac!

CECILE: T'as pas besoin de sacrer, Claude.

PAQUETTE: C'est correct. As-tu appelé Chez Momo pour faire venir de la bière?

CECILE: Oui, Claude.

JOHNNY: Hot, eh? Can't breathe in the fuckin' house. . . .
    Can't sleep.

PAQUETTE: Hey, don't talk about it. Today in work,
    one guy, he faints.

JOHNNY: Oh yeah?

PAQUETTE: At the machine. Just like that. There's one
    way to get the day off, eh?

JOHNNY: Ya got no air conditioning?

PAQUETTE: No, the bosses say there's some energy crisis
    or something, so they stop the air conditioning in the
    factory, eh? Not in the office, of course.

JOHNNY: Tell the union.

PAQUETTE: Hey, the union. It's too hot to laugh, câlice.

JOHNNY: Another fire last night, eh?

PAQUETTE: Ah, oui. What street?

JOHNNY: On Liverpool.

PAQUETTE: Liverpool encore. Tabarnac.

JOHNNY: Fuckin' firebugs, man. This block is gonna go
    up for sure.

PAQUETTE: Oui, that's for sure.

JOHNNY: Soon as I get my cheque, I'm gonna pull off a
    midnight move. Fuck this shit!

PAQUETTE: Oui, midnight move, for sure. Hey, just like the Arsenaults en bas. Fuck the landlords! It's the best way.

JOHNNY: Yeah . . . . . Whew, hot. Going anywhere this summer?

PAQUETTE: Moi? Balconville.

JOHNNY: Yeah. Miami Bench.

THIBAULT drives in on his Chez Momo's delivery bike.

THIBAULT: Chez Momo's is here.

JOHNNY: Hey, Thibault T-bone.

TOM: Hey, ya fixed the flat?

THIBAULT gets off his bike. He takes a case of beer from the bike.

THIBAULT: Oui. Hey, me, I know the bike, eh? I know what to do.

JOHNNY: Hey, T-bone.

THIBAULT: Chez Momo's is here.

Coming up the stairs, he trips on the broken step.

JOHNNY: Watch the step!

PAQUETTE: Watch the beer!

JOHNNY: You okay?

THIBAULT: Me? I'm okay. But my leg, I don't know.

PAQUETTE: Why don't you read the sign?

THIBAULT: Eh?

PAQUETTE: The sign. . . .

THIBAULT reads the sign on the balcony. It reads: "Prenez garde."

THIBAULT: Prenez garde. Okay, prenez garde. So what?
   Tiens, ta bière.

He puts the case of beer down next to PAQUETTE.
PAQUETTE gives him some money for the beer.

PAQUETTE: As-tu fini pour à soir?

THIBAULT: Oui, fini. C'est mon dernier voyage.

He shakes the change in his pocket.

THIBAULT: Hey, des tips.

JOHNNY: Had a good day, eh?

THIBAULT: Hey, Johnny. Johnny B. Good. Long time,
   no see, like they say.

JOHNNY: Yeah.

THIBAULT: Bye-bye, Johnny B. Good. You remember
   that?

JOHNNY: Remember what?

THIBAULT: Hey, there in the park, when they used to
   have the dances. You used to sing all the time like Elvis.

He does an imitation of Elvis.

THIBAULT: Tutti-fruiti, bop-bop-aloo, bop-a-bop,
   bam-boom. Like that, in the park.

JOHNNY: Yeah, yeah.

THIBAULT: C'était le fun. Me, I like that, but the girls grew up. They get old. You too. Paquette too. He's so fat now. Very fat.

PAQUETTE: Hey, hey.

JOHNNY: You remember all that shit?

THIBAULT: Me? Sure. I remember everything. Everything. Everybody forgets but me. I don't. It's funny, that, eh?

JOHNNY: Yeah.

THIBAULT: But you, you don't sing no more.

JOHNNY: No, I don't sing no more.

THIBAULT: Well, everybody gets old. It's funny, I watch it all change, but it's still the same thing . . . . I don't know. So what, eh?

PAQUETTE takes THIBAULT's nude magazine out of his back pocket and flips through it.

PAQUETTE: Hey, Thibault. You have a girlfriend?

THIBAULT: Me? Sure. I got two of them. Deux.

PAQUETTE: Deux?

THIBAULT takes back his magazine.

THIBAULT: Sure. I got one on Coleraine and the other one, she lives on Hibernia. Two girls. It's tough.

He comes down the stairs.

THIBAULT: English too. That surprise me. English, they do it too.

THIBAULT exits on his bike. PAQUETTE takes his beer and moves over to his balcony.

JOHNNY: *pointing to his head, referring to THIBAULT* The lights are on, but nobody's home.

PAQUETTE: He might as well be crazy, eh? It helps.

JOHNNY: Thinking's no good, man. I wish I could have half my brain removed. Boom! No more troubles. Just like Thibault.

CECILE: Pauvre homme. He was such a good boy when he was young. Remember?

PAQUETTE: It's easy to be good when you're young.

CECILE: He should have become a priest.

PAQUETTE: Cécile, nobody becomes a priest anymore.

He bumps into one of CECILE's plants.

CECILE: Claude, fais attention à mes plantes!

PAQUETTE: Toi, pis tes câlices de plantes. Y'en a partout sur le balcon.

IRENE enters. She is wearing her waitress uniform. She is coming home from work. She stops at MURIEL's house.

IRENE: Hi, Tommy. Your mother home?

TOM: Yeah.

IRENE: *knocking on MURIEL's door* Yoo-hoo, Muriel. It's me . . . . Pointe Action Committee meeting tonight at seven-thirty, eh?

MURIEL: *at the screen door*   I don't think I'll be going,
     Irene.

IRENE: It's an important meeting, Muriel. We're going
     down to the City Hall to demand more stop signs on the
     streets. Kids are getting hurt.

MURIEL: Yeah, I know.

IRENE: The more of us there, the better.

MURIEL: Yeah. I'm just not in the mood.

IRENE: You okay?

MURIEL: Yeah.

IRENE: Well, okay.

*She goes up the stairs, avoiding the broken step. MURIEL goes
back into her house.*

IRENE: Shit, why doesn't somebody fix that goddamn
     step?

JOHNNY: I didn't break it.

PAQUETTE: Hey, if I fix it, the landlord will raise the
     rent.

IRENE: *at the top of the stairs, looking at JOHNNY and
     his beer*   Having fun?

JOHNNY: Just having a couple of brews, Irene.

IRENE: Yeah, sure.

JOHNNY: *offering her a beer*   Here, have one.

She pushes his arm out of the way.

JOHNNY: Hey, don't get self-righteous, okay? I get bored, alright? Bored!

IRENE gives him his carton of cigarettes.

IRENE: Did you go down to the U.I.C.?

JOHNNY: "The cheque's in the mail," unquote.

IRENE: They said that last week.

JOHNNY: They'll say it again next week too. . . . Irene, relax. Have a brew.

IRENE: Let me by.

She goes into the house.

PAQUETTE: *from his balcony*   Hey, there's always trouble when a woman gets a job, eh?

JOHNNY: Yeah, fuckin' U.I.C., slave market, people lined up like sheep. I hate lines.

PAQUETTE: Me, I don't know what's worse, working or not working. Sometimes I wish they'd lay me off for maybe a month.

JOHNNY: Factory getting to ya?

PAQUETTE: Hey, I even dream of it at night, hostie. Click clack, bing bang, click clack, bing bang. It's bad enough being there in the day, but I see it at night too, hostie.

JOHNNY: Twelve weeks, I've been waiting for that cheque. . . four weeks penalty for getting fired, four weeks for filing the claim late, and another four weeks waiting for them to put the cheque in the fuckin' mail.

PAQUETTE: Hey, if they treat a dog like that, the S.P.C.A. would sue them.

DIANE enters. She is wearing shorts and high heels. She prances along in her high heels.

JOHNNY: Love that walk, Diane.

DIANE: Fuck you!

PAQUETTE: Hey, watch ton langage, toi.

DIANE climbs the stairs. When she has passed PAQUETTE, she turns and mouths the words, "Fuck you too." She goes into the house.

JOHNNY: *shouting after her*   Hey, you're gonna break a leg in those things.

PAQUETTE: Maudit.

JOHNNY: She's starting to look good.

PAQUETTE: Oui. Too good.

JOHNNY: Lots of nice young pussy around the neighbourhood, man. Breaks my heart to see it all.

PAQUETTE: *reaching for his wallet*   Johnny, I have something . . . .

He comes over and shows JOHNNY a photograph from his wallet.

PAQUETTE: Hey. Look at that . . . .

JOHNNY: Who's that? Cécile?

PAQUETTE: Oui . . . . She was nice, eh?

JOHNNY: Yeah.   *Looking at the photograph again.*
    Who's that?

PAQUETTE: That? That's me. Moi.

JOHNNY: You're not serious?

PAQUETTE: Hey. Okay, okay.

He snatches back his wallet and returns to his balcony.

*From DIANE's room, the record "Hot Child in the City," can
be heard.*

PAQUETTE: Hey, Cécile. . . . Cécile, dis à Diane de
    baisser sa musique de tuns.

CECILE: *shouting into the house*   Diane, baisse la
    musique juste un peu.

The volume goes down. The music fades away.

*IRENE comes out on her balcony to hang up her waitress
uniform. JOHNNY goes over to her and starts to hug her.*

IRENE: Stop it.

JOHNNY: Honey, don't be mad.

IRENE: I'm not mad, Johnny. Stop it. You smell of beer.

JOHNNY: Okay, I'll hold my breath, Irene.

IRENE: Johnny, you've got to do something. . . .
    Anything. . . . Keep yourself busy.

JOHNNY: Yeah. I'm gonna call up some people, try to
    get something together, as soon as I get my first cheque.

IRENE: That goddamn cheque!

JOHNNY: Well, I don't want to give up now. Those
            bastards owe me that money, Irene.

IRENE: Well, why don't you come down to our
            Unemployment Committee meetings?

JOHNNY: You know I don't like meetings.

IRENE: Yeah, yeah. Ya'd rather watch "Charlie's
            Angels."

JOHNNY: Irene, it's gonna be alright, okay? Say "okay."
            Say "okay."

IRENE: Okay.

JOHNNY: Alright.

IRENE: I don't know why I have to nag. I don't want to
            nag. Don't want to sound like my mother.

JOHNNY: Hey, what's the matter?

He starts to tickle her.

JOHNNY: You sensitive, eh? You sensitive?

IRENE: Johnny.

JOHNNY: Come on, a Québec quickie.

PAQUETTE: *from his balcony*   Hey, Jean. It's too hot
            for that, eh?

JOHNNY: Aw, the heat makes me horny. . . .

*An election campaign truck passes by playing Elvis Presley
music and broadcasting in French and English.*

VOICE: Vote for Gaëtan Bolduc. Gaëtan Bolduc's the man for you. The man of the people. Bolduc is on your side.

JOHNNY: Fuck you, Bolduc!

IRENE: Bolduc is on *his* side.

VOICE: Remember, on the 6th, vote for progress, vote for change, vote for a winner. Vote for Bolduc, the man for you... available and dynamic....

The sound fades away.

JOHNNY: Circus is starting early this year. A month away from the election and he's already doing his fuckin' number.

IRENE: Bolduc, the boss. Did ya see the size of his new house?

JOHNNY: Once a year, he buys hot dogs for the kids on the Boardwalk. Big fuckin' deal!

TOM: Yeah.... Stale hot dogs.

PAQUETTE: Those guys are all the same crooks.

IRENE: I don't know what's worse, Joe Who or René Quoi?

She goes and gets the mail.

PAQUETTE: Bolduc, he was okay... until he got the power. Then, that's it. He forgets us.

JOHNNY: Any mail for me?

IRENE: *looking through the mail*   No. Aw, shit. La merde.

JOHNNY: What?

IRENE: Water tax. Eighty-four dollars for water. Christ, it tastes like turpentine and they charge us like it's champagne.

JOHNNY: Hey, all the bills are in French anyhow, separatist bastards. Tell them we're paying in English.

PAQUETTE: Hey, I don't like that.

JOHNNY: What?

PAQUETTE: There's a lot of English bastards around too, eh?

JOHNNY: Yeah, but they're not forcing ya out of the province.

PAQUETTE: Learn how to speak French, that's all.

CECILE: You know, Irene, there was another fire last night.

IRENE: Another one?

CECILE: Oui. Last night. A big one.

IRENE: The Pointe Action Group thinks the landlords are setting the fires themselves.

PAQUETTE: The landlords? Burning down their own houses?

IRENE: For the insurance.

JOHNNY: Yeah, I believe that.

PAQUETTE: It's punk kids that do it. They got no father. The mother, she drinks in the taverns. What do they care, eh? They should make them work. Stop all the welfare.

IRENE: There is no work.

PAQUETTE: There's jobs, if they want them. They don't try hard enough.

JOHNNY: Yeah, there's jobs, but who wants to be a busboy all their lives?

PAQUETTE: It's a job.

JOHNNY: Yeah, well, I'm no fuckin' immigrant. I was born here.

PAQUETTE: That's the trouble...too many people. Overpopulation, they call it. We need another war or something. Stop all the welfare and make the lazy bums work.

IRENE: How come people always blame the poor? They never blame the rich.

PAQUETTE: Hey you, tell me, who's got the money, eh? Who's got all the money?

JOHNNY: Not me.

PAQUETTE: It's the English and the Jews.

IRENE: Hey!

PAQUETTE: They control everything, the goddamn Jews. That's the trouble.

IRENE: Hey, my mother was Jewish, so don't give me that shit, okay?

PAQUETTE: Hey, I don't talk about the good Jews. . . .

JOHNNY: What the fuck's going on?

PAQUETTE: Hey, me, I work all my life. All my life, me. Since I was ten years old.

JOHNNY: Yeah, so why cry about it?

PAQUETTE: Hey, John, that's not what I'm talking about.

JOHNNY: Hey, fuck the politics!

CECILE: Who knows what is true, eh? What is the truth?

PAQUETTE: You, you go light candles in the church. Me, I know what is the truth. A piece of shit, câlice.

CECILE: Claude.

PAQUETTE: Ah, oui. Claude.

IRENE: Anyhow, forget it.

JOHNNY: Yeah, fuck the politics. Nobody has fun in the Pointe anymore. We should have a party or something.

IRENE: A party, on what?

JOHNNY: Next week, I get my cheque, right? We'll have a party, just like the old days. Invite everybody on the block. We'll have a ball.

IRENE: You'll have a ball. I'll clean up the mess.

IRENE goes into the house.

JOHNNY: Irene, fuck!

He exits after her.

MURIEL: *from inside her house*   Tom, your supper's on the table.

TOM: Yeah, yeah.

MURIEL: *coming out of the house carrying a pot of spaghetti* Tommy, I'm not going to tell you again.

TOM: What is it? Spaghetti?

MURIEL: Yeah, spaghetti.

TOM: I'm not hungry. I don't want any.

MURIEL: You don't want it? You don't want it? Well, here, take it!

She dumps the spaghetti on TOM's head.

TOM: Ma! Shit!

He exits down the alley.

PAQUETTE: That woman, she's a little bit crazy, I think.

CECILE: T'as pas faim, Claude?

PAQUETTE: Y fait trop chaud. Fais-moi une limonade.

CECILE goes to get him a lemonade. DIANE comes out on the balcony and sits in the rocking chair. She is reading a magazine. PAQUETTE starts in on her.

PAQUETTE: Où est-ce que t'étais hier soir?

DIANE: Dehors.

PAQUETTE: Où ça dehors?

DIANE: Dehors. J't'ai dit dehors.

PAQUETTE: Dehors avec Jean-Guy pis toute la gang. Vous avez fumé, vous avez bu, vous avez fourré, vous avez eu du fun, hein?

DIANE: Oui, on a eu ben du fun.

PAQUETTE: Il est même pas pusher. Qu'est-ce qu'y fait pour vivre d'abord?

DIANE: Il travaille des fois. J'sais pas. Demande-lui si tu veux savoir.

PAQUETTE: Diane, tu vois pas que c'est un hostie de pas-bon.

DIANE: Parce que toi tu sais ce qui est bon pour moi. Tu t'es pas regardé.

PAQUETTE: Pis tu t'penses smart. Tu penses que t'as inventé le monde. Eh. Diane, regarde les femmes dans la rue. C'est ça que tu veux? Te marier, avoir un petit par année, devenir large de même, t'écraser devant la télévision, manger des chips et pis attendre le welfare et le mari. C'est ça que tu veux avec Jean-Guy?

DIANE: Tant qu'à ça pourquoi pas?

PAQUETTE: Bon. Ben tant que tu vas rester ici, tu vas rentrer à minuit. Tu vas à l'école. C'est pour te sortir de cette câlice de merde-là.

DIANE: Tu vas à l'école, pis y a même pas de job en sortant.

PAQUETTE: Diane, pense. Sers-toi de ta tête, pas de ton cul, crisse.

CECILE: *returning with a lemonade*   Claude.

PAQUETTE: Comment, Claude? Tabarnac, t'es sa mère, parles-y.

CECILE: Mais elle est jeune.

PAQUETTE: Oh. Oh, elle est jeune. Parce qu'est jeune, elle a droit de tout faire, pis quand elle va nous arriver en ballon.

DIANE: Fais-toi en pas, parce que j'prends la pillule.

She shows him her pill dispenser.

PAQUETTE: Maudit crisse.

He comes down the stairs and exits into the shed.

PAQUETTE: Va chez-toi.

CECILE: Tu l'as fait fâcher.

DIANE: Il est stupide.

CECILE: Mais, c'est ton père, Diane.

DIANE: Il est stupide pareil.

CECILE: Il essaye de t'aider. Y s'inquiète pour toi.

DIANE: Ça, Cécile, c'est ton problème. C'est pas le mien. J'suis pas obligée de l'endurer.

CECILE: C'est la job qui fait qu'y est fatigué. Y voudrait être fin avec toi des fois, mais il en peut plus, il est trop fatigué.

DIANE: Tu le gâtes trop, Cécile. C'est de ta faute. Tu le gâtes trop.

CECILE: Faut bien vivre.

DIANE: Dis-y donc non des fois, peut-être qu'il serait plus fin avec toi.

They hear a hammering noise coming from the shed.
PAQUETTE is in there working on his car.

DIANE: Regarde, y passe plus d'temps avec son maudit Buick qu'il en passe avec toi.

CECILE: Mon erreur moi-là, ç'a été d'avoir juste un enfant. Si tu te maries, Diane, arrange-toi pas pour avoir juste un enfant parce que tu vas te sentir bien toute seule.

DIANE: Maman, t'aurais dû rester au Lac St-Jean à la campagne avec ta famille. C'était là ta place, pas ici. C'est vrai, ça.

IRENE and JOHNNY come out of their house. IRENE is on her way to her Pointe Action Committee meeting.

IRENE: You wanna come to the meeting?

JOHNNY: No.

IRENE: Why not?

JOHNNY: 'Cause they're boring.

IRENE: Boring?

JOHNNY: Yeah, everybody's sitting around with a long face. . . . Boring!

IRENE: We're planning our next action.

JOHNNY: Yeah, sure. Another demonstration. Big fuckin' deal!

IRENE: We gotta start somewhere.

JOHNNY: Yeah, well, they got a long fuckin' ways to go.

IRENE comes down the stairs.

IRENE: If you're waiting for Superman, you're gonna wait a long, long time.

JOHNNY: If ya wanna fight politicians, go out and shoot a couple of them. All this talking drives me nuts.

He goes back into the house.

IRENE: *starting after him*   I'll be back at ten. There's some supper in the fridge.

IRENE sees MURIEL crying as she cleans up the spaghetti.

IRENE: Muriel, you okay? You alright, girl?

MURIEL: Oh, go away.

IRENE: What's wrong?... What's right? Guess that's an easier question, eh?

MURIEL: Oh, I feel stupid.

IRENE: Here, I got a kleenex.

MURIEL: Thanks.

IRENE: You're not pregnant, are ya?

MURIEL: Don't be crazy.

IRENE: Got the blues?

MURIEL: I'm worried about my stomach. It's acting up again.

IRENE: Maybe it's ulcers.

MURIEL: I don't know.

IRENE: Go to the hospital.

MURIEL: I'm afraid.

IRENE: You're afraid of what the doctor might say?

MURIEL: Yeah.

IRENE: Well, at least you'll know what you've got . . . . You'll feel better once you do.

MURIEL: I dunno.

IRENE: I'll go with ya.

MURIEL: Irene, you don't have to.

IRENE: Listen, I wouldn't want to go alone either. So, how about, uh, Tuesday?

MURIEL: I don't know. All they do is give ya pills, dope ya up and send ya back home again.

IRENE: Well, let them take a look at ya anyhow.

MURIEL: Tuesday?

IRENE: Yeah.

MURIEL: Sick or not, what's the difference?

IRENE: When is your old man due back from the boats?

MURIEL: Him? Oh, he's taking his time. Don't worry, he's in no hurry to come back. It's the perfect life for him. He can drink all he wants, screw around . . . and he gets paid for it.

IRENE: Well, still it'll be nice to have him back.

MURIEL: Come off it! And your old man isn't much better. I'd dump him so quick, it wouldn't be funny. You're too good for him, Irene.

IRENE: Oh, well, ya know how it is? Ya marry a prince and he turns into a frog.

MURIEL: Yeah, Bill was always great for a good time. But he was no good for nothing else.

IRENE: He still sends the cheques?

MURIEL: Yeah. Aw, it's nobody's fault. . . . Everybody's fault. . . . Ever think about what we'll be doing in ten years?

IRENE: Ten years? Ugh, I don't think about it. Maybe we'll win the Super Loto or something. . . . You know, you gotta get out of the house more. Ya make a lousy housewife. Try something else.

MURIEL: Like what?

IRENE: I don't know. School?

MURIEL: Jesus Christ, they threw me out of Grade 8 for punching out the teacher.

IRENE: Yeah, I remember that.

MURIEL: Yeah. Old man Breslin with the wandering hands.

IRENE: Pow, pow! Love it!

MURIEL: He had it coming.

IRENE: He sure did and you gave it to him. People still talk about it, eh? Sure.

MURIEL: Yeah, eh?

IRENE: Yeah. . . . Tuesday?

MURIEL: Yeah, Tuesday. . . . Thanks, Irene.

IRENE: Aw, us girls got to stick together, eh?

CECILE starts to water her plants. The water drips down on IRENE and MURIEL below.

IRENE: Aw, shit. When she's not feeding her Air Force, she's watering her jungle . . . . Bye.

IRENE exits.

The broadcast VOICE is heard again.

VOICE: Gaëtan Bolduc, the man for you. The man of today, the man of the people, the man who cares. Vote for action, vote for a winner, vote for Bolduc. Gaëtan Bolduc . . . available and dynamic . . . the man for you.

FIRST VOICE: *from the truck*   Yeah, yeah. Bolduc, Bolduc, Bolduc. Câlice, how many more times do we have to drive around the block?

SECOND VOICE: *from the truck*   We got three more hours, hostie.

FIRST VOICE: *from the truck*   That shithead, Bolduc. Bolduc. Me, I'm so sick of his fuckin' name. Bolduc, Bolduc. Fuck you, Bolduc! You cheap son of a bitch.

SECOND VOICE: *from the truck*   Next time, we'll ask for forty bucks a day.

FIRST VOICE: *from the truck*   Hey, fifty. Fifty bucks a day.

SECOND VOICE: *from the truck*   Oui, fifty.

FIRST VOICE: *from the truck*   Crisse, François. The speaker is still on. They can hear us.

SECOND VOICE: *from the truck*   The speaker? What? The speaker! Câlice.

The VOICES stop. Elvis Presley music comes back on.

Blackout.

Scene Four

It is night. The sound of rock music is heard. It is a record playing. DIANE, CECILE, IRENE, MURIEL, THIBAULT and TOM are dancing in the street.

THIBAULT: Hey, look. I got one. The mashed potato duck.

IRENE: Hey. Come on, everybody, make a circle. Take turns in the middle. Come on.

Diane steps into the circle and does a dance, then TOM takes his turn.

MURIEL: Move your feet. Move your feet.

THIBAULT: *stepping into the circle*   Hey, the duck. Look, I got one. The mashed potato duck.

They push him out of the circle.

IRENE: Hey, Cécile. Come on.

They push CECILE into the circle. She moves a bit. They applaud.

IRENE: Hey, shake that thing.

IRENE: Alright, Muriel. Come on, your turn. Come on.

MURIEL: Aw, that's kids' stuff.

IRENE: Come on.

Just as MURIEL starts to dance, the record ends.

MURIEL: Well, that's it.

THIBAULT: It's hot, eh? Hot . . . whew.

TOM: Hey. Where's Johnny?

IRENE: Him? He's always late. He's the star, right?

MURIEL: That's one word for him.

IRENE: Hey, Muriel. Tell that joke. The one you told me this morning.

MURIEL: Naw, naw. You tell it.

IRENE: Come on.

MURIEL: No. You tell it better.

IRENE: Okay. You ready? Okay, this guy is going to bed with a girl for the first time. . . .

THIBAULT: Oh, dirty joke! Hey!

MURIEL: Don't worry, Thibault. You'll never get it.

IRENE: Yeah, and he takes off his socks and shoes, and his feet are deformed, and she says, "What's wrong with your feet?" And he says, "Well, when I was a kid, I had toelio."

TOM: "Toelio."

IRENE: And she says, "You mean, polio." "No, toelio." And well, then, he takes off his pants. . . .

THIBAULT whistles.

MURIEL: Down, Thibault. Down.

IRENE: And . . . and his knees are all, you know, bulgy.

DIANE: C'est quoi ça, "bulgy?"

IRENE: Tout enflé. . . . And the girl says, "What's wrong
with your knees?" "Well, when I was a kid, I had the
kneasles." "You mean, measles." "No, kneasles." Then,
he takes off his underwear. . . .

THIBAULT whistles again.

IRENE: And she says, "Oh, no, don't tell me you had
smallcocks too." Small cocks.

They all laugh.

MURIEL: Thibault, ya got it now?

CECILE: Diane. "Smallcocks," c'est quoi?

DIANE: P'tite bizoune.

CECILE: Oh, bizoune. Oui.

MURIEL: Shit, it's been so long I forgot what they look
like.

The girls all laugh.

THIBAULT: Hey, that's funny, that, eh?

TOM: Hey, ya wanna see my Elvis Presley imitation? Eh?

DIANE: Oui.

TOM: Ya wanna see it?

MURIEL: No.

IRENE: Sure.

TOM: Okay? Ya ready?

IRENE: Ready.

TOM: Elvis!

He bends his head back and crosses his arms like a layed-out corpse. They all groan.

DIANE: I like that.

She copies his Elvis imitation.

DIANE: Elvis!

THIBAULT: That's all?

TOM: Yeah.

DIANE puts another record on. It is "Hot Child in the City." THIBAULT grabs her and begins to dance.

THIBAULT: Cha-cha-cha, hostie.

DIANE: Hey, not so close, okay? Not so close. J'vas te puncher.

THIBAULT: Hey, let's dance. Dansons.

IRENE: *cutting in*   Here, Diane. You take Tom.

She grabs THIBAULT. TOM and DIANE dance.

IRENE: Come on, Thibault, you sexy thing.

THIBAULT: Cha-cha-cha, hostie.

IRENE and THIBAULT dance.

IRENE: *turning to MURIEL*   Christ, hey Muriel, look. *Referring to her and THIBAULT.*   The last tango in the Pointe.

MURIEL: Careful. You'll get him so excited, he'll piss himself.

PAQUETTE and JOHNNY enter with their arms around one another's shoulders. They are drunk and singing.

PAQUETTE AND JOHNNY: *singing*
Jesus saves his money at
    the Bank of Montréal.
Jesus saves his money at
    the Bank of Montréal.
Jesus saves his money at
    the Bank of Montréal.
Jesus saves, Jesus saves —
    Jesus Saves.

IRENE: Shit, he's drunk already.

PAQUETTE: Hey, les femmes. Nous sommes ici.

DIANE mimics him.

THIBAULT: Hey, Paquette. Watch me dance.

JOHNNY: *singing with PAQUETTE*
Irene, goodnight,
Irene, goodnight,
Goodnight, Irene,
Goodnight, Irene,
I'll see you in my dreams.

PAQUETTE: Hey, les femmes. C'est moi.

JOHNNY: Hey, Irene. I'm a little late. Had a few drinks with what's his name.

PAQUETTE: Paquette.

JOHNNY: Pole-quette.

PAQUETTE: Naw. Paw-quette.

JOHNNY: Okay, tell the people your name *together*....
Paquette.

THIBAULT: Thibault. My name, Thibault.

*PAQUETTE and JOHNNY start to climb the stairs. JOHNNY
stumbles on the broken step.*

PAQUETTE: Eh, Johnny? Un autre p'tit step. La bière est
en haut.

IRENE: Fais attention à sa tête.

*She goes to help JOHNNY up the stairs. She is followed by
MURIEL, THIBAULT, DIANE and TOM.*

PAQUETTE: C'est sa tête carrée. C'est les coins qui
accrochent.

When JOHNNY gets up the stairs, he grabs IRENE.

JOHNNY: Irene, I love ya, love ya, love ya....

THIBAULT: We have fun, eh? Watch me dance.

JOHNNY: Yeah, we're gonna rock this joint. Where's the
beer?

MURIEL: You've had enough.

PAQUETTE: Hey, Johnny. Dansons, dansons.

He does a dance step.

JOHNNY: Where *is* everybody?

IRENE: This is it. We're all here.

JOHNNY: What do ya mean? Where are they? Danny?
    Jerry?

IRENE: Guess they couldn't make it.

JOHNNY: I knew the fuckers wouldn't come.

IRENE: Maybe they'll come later.

JOHNNY bangs into his house.

IRENE: Johnny. . . .

PAQUETTE: Put on some music. Hey, what's wrong?
    Put on some music. We'll have a good time.

He goes into his house and puts on the record; "Hot Child in the City."

THIBAULT: Tutti-fruiti, hostie. Let's twist some more.

JOHNNY: *inside his house*   What's Jerry's number?
    What's his fuckin' number?

IRENE: I dunno.

PAQUETTE: Hey, Diane. C'est ta tune.

PAQUETTE: *to MURIEL*   Hey, let's dance. . . . Why
    not?

MURIEL: Ask your wife.

PAQUETTE: Come on. I don't bite.

MURIEL: You're drunk.

They dance on the balcony.

PAQUETTE: Eh? Not bad, eh? I dance good, eh?

MURIEL: Yeah, sure. Terrific.

PAQUETTE: Not bad for a peasoup, eh?

JOHNNY: *inside the house, on the phone*   Jerry, that
    you? What are ya doing home? You're supposed to be
    here. . . . What? . . . Hey, turn that fuckin' music down. . . .
    What? . . . Fuck that shit, man. This is supposed to be a
    get together and nobody's here. Nobody! Just the Pepsi's
    next door. . . . What? . . . What? . . . I don't want to hear
    that shit, Jerry. You coming? You coming? . . . Maybe
    later? Fuck you!

*He slams down the receiver and bangs his way out onto the
balcony.*

IRENE: Johnny. Johnny. . . .

JOHNNY: The party's over. Fuck off! Everybody, fuck off!

PAQUETTE: Hey, Jacques. We'll have a good time, eh?

JOHNNY pushes PAQUETTE.

JOHNNY: Get on your own fuckin' side.

PAQUETTE: Hey. Hey.

JOHNNY: Fuckin' gorf. Pepper. Get on your own side.

PAQUETTE: Hey, watch that, eh? Fais attention, okay?

JOHNNY: We were here first, ya fuckin' farmer. Go back
    to the sticks.

PAQUETTE: Hey, reste tranquille, eh?

JOHNNY: Ya wanna fight? Wanna fight?

JOHNNY *swings at PAQUETTE, but misses him. He falls down. IRENE and MURIEL push him towards the door of his house.*

PAQUETTE: Keep your garbage on your side.

JOHNNY: *mumbling*   The party's over. No more parties. No more.

IRENE: Get him into the house.

MURIEL: Stupid men.

They carry him into his house.

JOHNNY: Jerry. Where's Jerry? Jerry?

MURIEL: Good old days. . . . Never was any good old days.

They exit into the house.

THIBAULT: Johnny, he gets a little drunk tonight, eh?

TOM: Hey, a little.

DIANE: It's fun for them. That's the way they have fun.

CECILE: It's a full moon. That's why everyone is so crazy.

PAQUETTE: What's wrong? Hey, what's wrong?

He puts the record back on. It is "Hot Child in the City" once again.

THIBAULT: Away, Paquette. Let's twist some more.

TOM: *to MURIEL, as she comes out of JOHNNY's house*
Is he okay?

MURIEL: He's okay. You wanna end up just like him?
    That's the way you're going.

TOM: Yeah, yeah.

*PAQUETTE goes over to MURIEL, who isn't interested in
dancing, so he starts dancing with DIANE. He begins to
slobber all over her. She pushes him away, goes down the stairs
and exits down the lane.*

CECILE: Diane. Diane.

PAQUETTE: Who wants to dance? Hey.

He heads towards MURIEL.

MURIEL: Get lost. Beat it.

She pushes him aside.

PAQUETTE: Quoi?

MURIEL: Ya make me sick.

PAQUETTE: Hey, parle-moi en français, eh? Parle-moi
    en français.

MURIEL: Go on. Hit me. Hit me. Try it.

PAQUETTE: Maudits anglais. How come I got to speak
    English, eh? How come?

MURIEL: 'Cause you're stupid.

PAQUETTE: Maudits anglais. Throw them all out.
    Toute le gang. On est au Québec. On est chez-nous.

MURIEL: I was born here too, ya bigmouth Frenchman.

PAQUETTE: It's our turn now, eh? Our turn. And
    Ottawa, Ottawa can kiss my Pepsi ass.

MURIEL: Ferme ta gueule, toi.

THIBAULT: Fuck the Queen!

MURIEL: Fuck Lévesque!

MURIEL goes back into IRENE's house. PAQUETTE knocks over one of CECILE's plants by accident.

CECILE: Claude, fais attention à mes plantes. Claude.

PAQUETTE picks up one of her plants and throws it over the railing.

PAQUETTE: Tiens, ta câlice de plante.

CECILE runs into the house crying.

PAQUETTE: It's crying time again, eh? Crying time again.

He opens another beer.

THIBAULT: Me, I don't hate the English. I just don't like them, that's all.

PAQUETTE: Maudits anglais!

THIBAULT: They got funny heads. Square heads.

PAQUETTE: *to TOM*   You. Hey, you. Think maybe you got a chance, eh? No more. That's one good thing now. We're all the same now, eh? We're all equal. Nobody's got a chance. Nobody.

THIBAULT: Fuck the Queen!

PAQUETTE: Maybe you got dreams, eh? Me too. I had dreams. Thibault too. He had dreams.

THIBAULT: Oui, me too.

PAQUETTE: If you knew what I know, you'd go jump in the river right now. Tonight.

THIBAULT: Oui, tonight. The river. No joke, that.

PAQUETTE hugs THIBAULT.

PAQUETTE: Thibault, you're a bum . . . a bum and a drunk.

THIBAULT: Oui, a bum.

PAQUETTE: You know what? Me, I work all my life. All my life.

THIBAULT: That's too bad.

PAQUETTE: When I was young, I was going to do this and that, but the job, the fuckin' job, it took my life away. What can you do? Everybody says, "What can you do?" That's the way it goes.

THIBAULT: That's the way it goes.

PAQUETTE: You get the old and ugly and you die . . . and that's all.

THIBAULT: That's all.

PAQUETTE: I try, but it don't help. No matter what you do.

TOM comes down the stairs and goes into his house to get his guitar.

PAQUETTE: No matter what you do.

THIBAULT: So what? That's what I say. So what?

PAQUETTE: So what? Maudits anglais.

THIBAULT: Oui. So what?

He looks into the case of beer.

THIBAULT: Hey. No more beer.

IRENE and MURIEL come out on the balcony.

THIBAULT: Eh, y a plus de bière?

PAQUETTE: On va aller en chercher en ville.

THIBAULT: Comment?

PAQUETTE: Ben . . . avec mon char.

THIBAULT: Ton char?

PAQUETTE: Ben oui. Mon char, hostie.

They come down the stairs.

THIBAULT: Ah, oui. Ton char dans le garage. Prenez
    garde. Watch the step.

They pick up some tools and exit for the shed, to fix the car.

IRENE: They're gonna get themselves killed.

MURIEL: Don't worry, they'll never get that car to start.

IRENE: Well, Johnny's out for the night. He'll wake up
    tomorrow, drink a bottle of Coke and ask me what he did.

MURIEL: He needs a kick in the ass . . . and fast.

IRENE: He told me he wants me to find another man . . . .
    Yeah . . . . Here I am, thirty-four years old, and he wants
    me to go find another man. Fat chance.

MURIEL: I dunno. You're still in pretty good shape.

IRENE: Aw, I'm no spring chicken anymore. . . . I'm a broiler.

MURIEL: You're better off without a man. Who needs them?

IRENE: Aw, I guess I love the creep.

MURIEL: Love? Love never got through the Wellington Tunnel.

IRENE: I had this guy who was nuts about me. . . always phoning me up, calling on me. He's a teacher now in N.D.G. . . . But I fell for Johnny. He was a rebel. A real teen angel, ya know what I mean?

MURIEL: Yeah, so they grow up to be drunks.

IRENE: I can't blame him. He's been trying.

MURIEL: No, guess you can't blame the poor ignorant stupid bastards.

IRENE: I'm scared for him.

MURIEL: It never pays to be too nice, Irene. I used to be nice, but it never got me nowhere.

IRENE: Yeah. . . . But why, Muriel? Why? How do you change it?

MURIEL: They're all the same, Irene. . .all of them.

IRENE: The doctor's still taking tests?

MURIEL: Yeah. . . . You know doctors. They never tell ya nothing. All they do is poke your stomach, take your blood, give ya some pills and tell ya to come in next week. Makes ya feel like a goddamn guinea pig.

IRENE: Yeah, well, meanwhile there's the late movie, eh?
    What's on anyhow?

MURIEL: I dunno.

IRENE: See ya . . . .

MURIEL: Yeah, Irene . . . . Don't let him walk on you.
    That's what I'm trying to say anyhow.

IRENE: 'Night.

MURIEL: Yeah.

*IRENE goes into her house. MURIEL comes down the stairs.
She sees TOM sitting on her balcony with his guitar.*

MURIEL: I'm locking the door at twelve o'clock.

TOM: Yeah.

MURIEL: I mean it.

TOM: Yeah, yeah.

MURIEL goes into her house.

PAQUETTE: *yelling at THIBAULT in the shed*   Non,
    non. Le wrench. Donne-moi le wrench qui est sur la
    valise.

THIBAULT: La valise.

PAQUETTE: Oui, tabarnac.

THIBAULT: Y fait noir. Ouch!

PAQUETTE: Le hood. Fais attention au hood. Ta tête.

A slamming sound is heard.

PAQUETTE: Maudit, tabarnac de câlice de Sainte
    Vierge. Hostie, que t'es cave! Tiens la lumière.

THIBAULT: La lumière. Okay.

TOM: *playing his guitar and singing*
    Tell you, Mona, what I'm gonna do,
    Build a house next door to you,
    Then I can see you in the summertime,
    We can blow kisses through the blinds.
    Come on, Mona, out in the front,
    Listen to my heart go bumpetity-bump.

*DIANE enters. When TOM has finished playing, she
applauds.*

TOM: Uh, hi.... Want some beer?... Go ahead, I got an
    extra bottle.

DIANE takes a sip of beer.

TOM: The party's over, eh?

DIANE: The party? Oui.

TOM: Uh... everybody got drunk and crazy, eh?

DIANE: Quoi?

TOM: Drunk, crazy.... Like that....

He mimes "drunk."

DIANE: Drunk? Ah, oui.... Mon anglais est pas tellement
    bon.

TOM: My French is, uh... comme ci, comme ça....
    Like that.... So, uh... what's new?

DIANE: What's new?

TOM: Yeah, new.

DIANE: You tell me?. . . Bon?. . . Well?

She moves towards the stairs.

TOM: Hey, uh. . . where ya going?

DIANE: I don't speak the good English.

TOM: Look, finish your beer. I mean, uh. . . . Why not?. . .

She stops at the foot of the stairs.

DIANE: I don't want to go home.

TOM: Yeah, I know the feeling. You, uh. . . never look too happy.

DIANE: Happy? What's that?. . . Something on TV?

TOM: Yeah, well, I dunno. . . . You're so pretty. Ya should be happy.

DIANE groans.

TOM: That's a dumb thing to say, eh? Yeah. . . . So, uh. . . . What do you do?

DIANE: Me? I still go to school. . . . I write poems sometimes.

TOM: Yeah, that figures. . . . Uh. . . . What kind of poems?

DIANE: Sad ones.

TOM: I'm asking 'cause, well...ya look like a girl who
         writes poems. Guess I could do it too, but I wouldn't know
         why. I flunked English. French too....Babysitting, that's
         all school is....

DIANE: Do you like films?...Me, I like films. But they
         make me feel bad too. I don't want them to stop.

TOM: Hey, cinemascope. In living colour, Diane
         Paquette.

DIANE: No, I'll never use that name. Not Paquette.

TOM: Okay. Diane, uh....

DIANE: Diane Desmarchais. Why not Diane
         Desmarchais?

TOM: Yeah. Okay. Boulevard Desmarchais. Sounds
         good....

DIANE: So, you don't go to school no more?

TOM: Naw. I mean, I know my ABC's...most of
         them....Looking for work....I dunno, it's crazy. I mean,
         if someone wanted me to work for them, why don't they
         ask me. I mean, I don't know why I've got to go looking
         for work when I don't even want it.

DIANE: No job, no money. No money, no nothing.

TOM: Yeah, money....Hey, uh....Don't you ever blink?

DIANE: Never.

TOM: Once a year or what?...

DIANE: Your hair, it makes you look funny.

TOM: Funny? What do you mean?

DIANE: I think it's too short.

TOM: Oui, too short.

DIANE: I think you have to grow it longer. . . .

TOM: Yeah, well, I'm getting out. I'm leaving. . . . Ever
           think of doing that? Goodbye Pointe Saint-Charles.

DIANE: Where will you go?

TOM: I dunno. . . anywhere. New York City.

DIANE: New York City?

TOM: Yeah, sure.

DIANE: They got jobs down there?

TOM: I dunno. . . . It's a big place. Ya never know. I
           might find a job as a musician, ya know? Once I learn
           about, uh, major chords, minor chords. Shit like that. . . .

DIANE: Well, salut. Bonne chance.

DIANE starts to go up the stairs.

TOM: Hey, Diane. Wait. Attends peu. . . . You wanna
           come with me?

DIANE: Avec toi? Pourquoi?

TOM: Well, I figure you wanna get out too. . . . Anyhow,
           forget it. It's stupid. Ya don't even know me. . . . I'm a
           bit stoned. . . . Well, see ya.

DIANE: Bye. . . . Write me a letter, okay?

She goes into her house.

TOM: Aw, forget it. It's stupid. . . stupid.

TOM exits with his guitar.

PAQUETTE and THIBAULT are heard banging away in the shed.

PAQUETTE: Verrat de tabarnac de crisse de ciboire.

THIBAULT: J'pense que c'est pas le spark plug, eh?

PAQUETTE: Fuck you. Où est le pipe wrench?

THIBAULT: Le pipe wrench?

PAQUETTE: Oui, le pipe wrench. Je pense que j'l'ai laissé sur le balcon.

THIBAULT: Le balcon. Okay, okay, okay, okay. Okay, so what?

He comes in from the shed and goes up the stairs. While he is looking for the pipe wrench, he drinks some beer from some discarded beer bottles.

THIBAULT: Le pipe wrench, le pipe wrench. So what? On se rendra jamais en ville.

PAQUETTE: Thibault. . . . Hostie. . . .

THIBAULT: Oui, j'cherche. J'cherche.

He takes a slug of beer from one of the beer bottles and gags on a cigarette butt.

THIBAULT: Agh. Touf. Une cigarette, hostie.

PAQUETTE gets the car started, guns the engine, then chokes it.

PAQUETTE: Tu veux pas partir. Tu veux pas partir. Ben. J'vas t'arranger ça.

PAQUETTE takes a hammer to the car. The sound of smashing is heard. CECILE comes out on her balcony.

CECILE: Mais, qu'est-ce qui se passe?...Claude?...

PAQUETTE comes out of the shed carrying a hammer. He throws the hammer to the ground and climbs the stairs.

THIBAULT: *to PAQUETTE*   You fix it?

PAQUETTE: *to CECILE*   Pas un mot s'a game. Pas un mot.

PAQUETTE and CECILE exit into their house, leaving THIBAULT standing alone on the balcony.

THIBAULT: Okay, on ira jamais en ville. So what? Thibault, he's okay. I go find my own beer. So what?

He comes down the stairs and exits. MURIEL comes out on her balcony.

MURIEL: Tommy, I'm gonna lock this door. Tommy?... Alright.

She shuts the door and bolts it closed.

Blackout.

Act Two
Scene One

It is night. JOHNNY and THIBAULT enter singing. Both of them are drunk. JOHNNY is riding THIBAULT's delivery bike.

JOHNNY AND THIBAULT: *singing*
>We don't care about
>All the rest of Canada,
>All the rest of Canada,
>All the rest of Canada.
>We don't care for
>All the rest of Canada,
>We're from Pointe Saint-Charles.

MURIEL: *from inside her house*   Shut up out there!

JOHNNY: Fuck you!

THIBAULT: So what, eh? Get off my bike, you . . . .
Away.

JOHNNY gets off of THIBAULT's bike.

JOHNNY: Hey, Thibault, you're not a separatist, are ya?

THIBAULT: FLQ, moi. Boom! I blow everything up.
    Boom!

He kicks a garbage can.

MURIEL: *from inside her house*   Jesus Murphy.

THIBAULT: *taking a magazine out of his back pocket*
    We have a good time, eh? Good time. Look, big tits.

He sits down on a bench. JOHNNY sits down beside him.

JOHNNY: You're my friend, eh, Thibault?

THIBAULT: Sure, if that's what you say.

JOHNNY: You're my only, only friend.

THIBAULT: I'm your only friend . . . and I'm not even
    your friend.

JOHNNY: So, whose friend are ya?

THIBAULT: I don't know.

JOHNNY: ·   You wanna know whose friend you are? You're
    my friend.

THIBAULT: Sure . . . . My mother, once she takes me to
    the Oratoire, because I got the polio. So, she takes me
    there. She prays to Saint Joseph, but the polio, it don't
    go away . . . .

JOHNNY: Fuck off.

THIBAULT: Eh, so what?

JOHNNY: What, so what?

THIBAULT: What so what?

JOHNNY: Yeah, you say, "So what?" and I say, "What so what?"

THIBAULT: You crazy, you.

JOHNNY: Fuckin' right, I'm crazy. *He begins to yell.* I'm trying, Irene. I'm trying. . . . I'm dying.

THIBAULT: Hey, Johnny. Do Elvis. Do Elvis. . . . "I'm all shook up."

JOHNNY: *snapping into an Elvis imitation* "I'm all shook up."

IRENE comes out on her balcony.

IRENE: Johnny.

JOHNNY: Irene, remember me when I was eighteen?

He does his Elvis imitation.

JOHNNY: "Be-bop-a-lula."

IRENE: Come on up to bed, Johnny. I've got to work tomorrow.

JOHNNY: Tomorrow? Fuck tomorrow! Everybody's worried about tomorrow. I'm worried about right now.

THIBAULT: Hey, do Elvis. Do some more Elvis. . . . "You ain't nothing but a hound dog."

JOHNNY: Elvis is dead, ya dumb Pepsi. He's dead. Don't ya understand that? He's dead.

He goes to the stairs and starts to climb them. He collapses.

IRENE: Come on, Johnny.

She comes down and tries to get him up the stairs. He grunts.

IRENE: Shit. La merde. . . . Muriel? Muriel?

MURIEL: *from inside her house*   I'm asleep.

IRENE: Muriel, give me a hand, will ya?

MURIEL: *from inside her house*   Leave him there, it'll do him good.

CECILE: *coming out on her balcony*   Madame, you need some help?

IRENE: Thanks.

CECILE comes down the stairs. Together, she and IRENE carry JOHNNY up the stairs and into his house.

JOHNNY: Irene, I love you. . . . Gonna buy ya a house, Irene.

CECILE comes back out. She sees THIBAULT sitting on the steps looking at one of his magazines.

THIBAULT: Paquette, Paquette, tu t'souviens? Toi et moi à la Rodéo? Big Fat Babette. . . . "Please Help Me I'm Falling in Love with You." Big tits. . . big tits.

CECILE: Shhhhhh, Thibault. Claude dort.

THIBAULT: *looking at his magazine*   Tits. . . big tits.

He rips a page out of the magazine. He goes and sits on his bike.

IRENE comes out on the balcony carrying two Cokes.

IRENE: Veux-tu un Coke, Cécile?

CECILE: Yes, that would be nice.

CECILE sits down on her rocking chair. IRENE comes and sits down beside her.

CECILE: It's so quiet, eh? This is my favourite time, when it's quiet.

IRENE: Yeah.

CECILE: Look, there's the Big Dipper.

IRENE: Oh yeah?

CECILE: Right there. Right next to that shed.

IRENE: You know, I haven't looked at the sky in years.

CECILE: When I was a little girl in Lac St-Jean, I knew the names of all the stars. . . the Great Bear, the Swan, the Hunter. . . .

IRENE: They've got names, eh?

CECILE: Of course. Everything has a name.

IRENE: How did you meet Paquette? Uh. . . Claude?

CECILE: He had a truck. He was a truck driver. . . . So handsome. . . . At first, we thought he would marry one of my older sisters, but she didn't want him because he was too loud. . . . And my mother too, she didn't like him. But. . . .

IRENE: You liked him.

CECILE: I was a young girl. . . .

IRENE: So was I. . . . I had a dream last night. . . .

CECILE: A dream? Tell me. I love dreams.

IRENE: I. . . .I dreamed I saw Jacob wrestling the angel. Imagine that.

CECILE: Jacob?

IRENE: Yeah, you know? Jacob . . . in the Bible.

CECILE: Jacob. Ah, oui.

IRENE: Anyhow, I woke up feeling good.

IRENE: Well, it's been one of those years, eh?

CECILE: Johnny and Claude, right now . . . they not getting along so good?

IRENE: Well, they're both being stupid. But Johnny started it. He's such a goddamn redneck sometimes.

CECILE: It's strange. . . . Before, Claude, he wants to be like the English . . . and now, he puts everything on them.

DIANE enters.

CECILE: Diane, il est passé minuit. Ton père va être fâché.

DIANE comes up the stairs.

DIANE: Irene, I have something . . . .

IRENE: Oh?

DIANE: Une lettre de Tom.

IRENE: Tom? He wrote you?

DIANE: Oui, but I can't understand all the words.

IRENE: Let me see it.

She takes the letter and looks at the postmark.

IRENE: Ormstown? What's the silly bugger doing in
           Ormstown?. . . You want me to read it?

DIANE: Oui.

IRENE: "Hi, Diane. . . . Took me a day hitchhiking to get
           this far so far. Tomorrow, guess I'll reach the border and
           cross over into the land of Jimmy Carter and Mickey
           Mouse."

DIANE laughs.

DIANE: Mickey Mouse.

IRENE: "I can feel New York City down there, pulling me
           like a magnet." Tu comprends? Magnet?

*IRENE mimes "magnet," banging the fist of one hand into her
other hand.*

DIANE: Oui.

IRENE: "Pull at him." Shit, it's gonna hit him on the
           head.

DIANE: Quoi?

IRENE: Uh. . .okay. "I don't have no money, but a faggot
           bought me a meal." Faggot? C'est un tapette.

DIANE: Oui.

IRENE: "I'm glad we had that talk, even if I did sound
           kind of crazy. . . . I think you're beautiful. I mean, how do
           you say something like that? But, it's true." Wow! Hot
           stuff!

DIANE takes back the letter.

DIANE: It's okay. . . . I understand the rest.

IRENE: Hey, sounds like Tom really likes ya, girl.

DIANE: Hey, I know what he wants.

IRENE: Yeah, so is he gonna get some?

DIANE: He's cute. . . a bit.

IRENE: New York City.

DIANE: Me, I want to go there.

IRENE: Yeah?

DIANE: Sure. Go there and live like in the movies. It would be fun, eh?

IRENE: Yeah. . . like the movies. Poor Muriel.

DIANE: His mother?. . . What for?. . . She was going to throw him out anyhow.

IRENE: Well, I've got to work tomorrow. Bye.

DIANE: Bye.

CECILE: Goodnight, Irene.

IRENE exits into her house.

CECILE: Diane, viens-tu te coucher?

DIANE: Non.

CECILE exits into her house.

DIANE sits at the top of the stairs. THIBAULT is still sitting on his bike at the bottom of the stairs.

THIBAULT: Diane. Diane.

DIANE: Va-t'en chez-vous, Thibault.

THIBAULT: Eh, Diane? J'vas m'acheter une Honda 750.
C'est vrai, Diane. Brammmmm, brammmmm. Honda.
J'vas m'en acheter une.

DIANE: Oui, oui.

THIBAULT: J'vas t'faire des rides, eh?

DIANE: Va-t'en chez-vous, Thibault.

THIBAULT: C'est vrai, Diane. Une 750. Brammmmm,
brammmmm.

*He exits on his bike. DIANE remains at the top of the stairs
looking at her letter.*

Blackout.

Scene Two

*The next day. It is a very hot Sunday afternoon. JOHNNY,
PAQUETTE and DIANE are on the balcony watching the
ballgame on TV—on separate TV's. MURIEL is sweeping her
balcony.*

JOHNNY: *watching TV*   Aw, shit . . . bunch of bums!

PAQUETTE: *watching TV*   Maudits Expos!

*IRENE enters yawning. She is wearing her waitress uniform.
She is coming home from work. She sees MURIEL sweeping
her balcony.*

IRENE: Boy, this heat . . . .

MURIEL: Couple more days of this and we'll be having riots.

IRENE: Yeah.

MURIEL: Sorry about last night. . . . I was in one of my moods.

IRENE: Aw, forget it. Hey, Diane got a letter from Tom, eh? . . . Yeah.

MURIEL: He writes to her, but he doesn't write to his mother?

IRENE: He's in Ormstown.

MURIEL: Ormstown? Where's that?

IRENE: Somewhere in the bush.

MURIEL: Well, as soon as he gets hungry, he'll come home. . . . Just let him try to get through the door.

IRENE: Aw, don't worry. Young guys are like tomcats. They always land on their feet.

MURIEL: Who says I'm worried?

IRENE: Okay.

PAQUETTE: *watching TV* Away, away . . . câlice.

JOHNNY: *watching TV* Aw, shit! Le merde! Move your ass! Move your ass!

PAQUETTE: *watching TV* Il est temps, tabarnac!

JOHNNY sees IRENE coming up the stairs.

JOHNNY: Hey, did ya pick me up some smokes?

IRENE dumps a pack of smokes in his lap and goes on into the house. CECILE enters. She is wearing her church clothes. She comes up behind MURIEL.

CECILE: Bonjour, Madame Williams.

MURIEL: *jumping in fright*   Oh God, don't creep up on me like that.

CECILE: How are you?...Nice day, eh?

MURIEL: Too hot.

CECILE: Ah, yes, too hot.... It's so nice to see people together in the church. Being together makes people feel so good.

PAQUETTE AND JOHNNY: *together*   Grimsley, ya bum!...Aux douches!

MURIEL: Yeah....   *Looking at where CECILE is standing.*   Move....

CECILE moves and MURIEL continues sweeping. CECILE goes up the stairs. DIANE notices her hat.

DIANE: Maman, les femmes n'ont plus besoin de porter de chapeau pour aller à la messe.

CECILE: Je sais, Diane, mais je suis habituée de même.

PAQUETTE and JOHNNY both react to something on the baseball game on TV.

CECILE: Diane, tu devrais venir avec moi dimanche prochain.

DIANE: C'est toujours le même show. Quand ils changeront le programme, peut-être que j'irai.

PAQUETTE: *to CECILE and DIANE*   Tabarnac, y
a-tu moyen d'écouter ma game tranquille? Ça fait une
semaine que j'attends après ça. Cécile, va me chercher
une bière.

CECILE: Oui, Claude. . . .

She goes to get him a beer.

JOHNNY: Hey, Irene?. . . Irene?. . .

IRENE: *at the screen door*   Yeah?

JOHNNY: Get me a Coke.

IRENE: What's the matter, you break your leg?

JOHNNY: It's too hot to move.

IRENE: I'm moving.

PAQUETTE: *watching TV*   Merde!

JOHNNY: *watching TV*   Shit!

PAQUETTE: Un autre foul ball, hostie!

CECILE brings PAQUETTE a beer.

CECILE: Claude, veux-tu un sandwich?

PAQUETTE: Quoi?

CECILE: Un sandwich?

PAQUETTE: *watching TV*   Away. . . away là!

She goes to get him a sandwich.

JOHNNY: *watching TV*   Faster! Get under it! Get
under it!. . . No, fuck!

PAQUETTE: *watching TV*   Shit! La merde!

*CECILE comes back and puts a sandwich in one of
PAQUETTE's hands and a beer in his other hand.*

DIANE: Paquette est assez grand pour se mouvoir tout
seul, Cécile.

PAQUETTE: Cécile. . . . C'est ta mère que t'appelles
Cécile. Tu vas me faire le plaisir de l'appeler Maman.

DIANE: *to PAQUETTE*   You are a piece of shit.

*She throws a bag of potato chips at him and stomps off into the
house.*

PAQUETTE: Voyons. Qu'est-ce qu'y lui prend?

CECILE: J'sais pas. J'pense qu'elle s'est chicané avec sa
chum.

JOHNNY: *watching TV*   Go, go, go!

PAQUETTE: *watching TV*   Vite, vite, vite! . . . Bonne.
That's it. . . . Oui.

JOHNNY: *watching TV*   About time. . . .

*Inside the House, DIANE puts on a record. It is "Hot Child in
the City."*

PAQUETTE: Cécile, dis-lui de baisser sa câlice de
musique de hot child in the city, hostie.

*CECILE goes into the house. The music fades away. IRENE
comes out and hands JOHNNY a Coke.*

IRENE: Johnny, I want to talk to you.

JOHNNY: Yeah, yeah.

IRENE: What happened last night?

JOHNNY: Last night?...Hey, I'm watching the game.

IRENE: When does it end?

JOHNNY: Eh?...Ten minutes.

IRENE: I want to talk to you before I go out.

JOHNNY: Yeah, yeah...talk. Okay.

IRENE: I mean it.

JOHNNY: Don't do the martyr, okay? Not the martyr, please.

IRENE exits into the house. THIBAULT enters on his bike. He starts putting "Gaëtan Bolduc...available and dynamic" campaign posters all over the walls.

MURIEL: *watching THIBAULT*   What's this?

THIBAULT: Dix piastres pour la journée....Me and four other guys are putting them up all over. Bolduc, he wants to win this time, eh?

MURIEL: *ripping down one of the posters*   Not on my wall....

THIBAULT: Eh? Not on your wall?

MURIEL: No.

THIBAULT: No?

MURIEL: No, you stupid little jerk.

She crumples up the poster and throws it at him.

THIBAULT: No?...Okay, no.

He goes up the stairs with his posters. He sees PAQUETTE and JOHNNY watching TV. He sits beside PAQUETTE.

THIBAULT: Hey, c'est quoi l'score? What's the score?

PAQUETTE: Huit à cinq.

JOHNNY: *shouting across at them* The Expos got five.

THIBAULT: Hey. Good game, eh?...Hot, eh? Hot... very hot. Très chaud....Agh...hard to breathe. *He coughs.* Agh, my throat....Hot....

PAQUETTE: *calling to CECILE* Cécile, apporte-moi deux autres bières.

CECILE: *at the screen door* Deux?

PAQUETTE: Oui.

THIBAULT: Ah, oui....Good game, eh?

PAQUETTE: Ferme ta gueule, toi. Okay?

THIBAULT: Hey, regarde.

He shows PAQUETTE a poster.

PAQUETTE: Ote-toi d'là. C'est quoi ça? Bolduc?

THIBAULT: Oui. Prends-en une.

PAQUETTE: Tu vas laisser tes cochonneries ailleurs.

He crumples up the poster and throws it over the balcony.

THIBAULT: Eh, tu votes pas Libéral cette année?

MURIEL: *from downstairs* Hey....Watch the garbage, okay?

CECILE brings out two beer.

CECILE: Ah, bonjour, Thibault. Comment va ta mère?

THIBAULT: Oui, ça va bien.

JOHNNY: *watching TV*   Slide, for fuck's sake! Slide!

PAQUETTE: *watching TV*   C'est pas un coursier, c'est un cheval de labo!

CECILE: Claude, j'aurais besoin de cinq piastres.

PAQUETTE: Cinq piastres, pourquoi? Diane? Dis-y de venir les demander à sa piece of shit, okay?

CECILE exits into the house.

THIBAULT: *looking at both TVs*   Hey, hey, it's the same game! The same game!

The broadcast VOICE is heard again.

VOICE: N'oubliez pas dans deux semaines, votez Gaëtan Bolduc. Bolduc est sur votre côté, toujours disponible et dynamique. . . . Bolduc. . . .

The broadcast truck plays Elvis Presley music. The music fades away.

THIBAULT: *referring to the broadcast VOICE*   Oui, that's him right there.

PAQUETTE: *watching TV*   Maudit, même pas capable de regarder sa game tranquille.

THIBAULT: *watching TV*   Trois hommes sur les buts.

PAQUETTE: *watching TV*   Y sont capables, si y veulent.

IRENE comes out on the balcony.

IRENE: Can we talk now?

JOHNNY: Shit, it bugs me when goofs like Bolduc use good Elvis music.

IRENE: Johnny, you got drunk again last night.

JOHNNY: Yeah. . . .

IRENE: Four nights in a row. . . . You said you were gonna stop. I thought we had all that settled.

JOHNNY: Listen. . . . This is not the right time.

IRENE: It is never the right time. I'm tired of waiting for the right time. Let's talk now. . . . Let's try to talk.

JOHNNY: Talk. . . . Look, I just need one more night to straighten out.

IRENE: Straighten out what?

JOHNNY: I'm not working, so you think you can pick on me, is that it? Is that it?

IRENE: This is not a contest.

JOHNNY: I got a hangover. . . . I'm in a bad mood.

IRENE: So, you're gonna go out tonight too?

JOHNNY: Yeah, that's right. . . . Yeah.

IRENE: Well, don't count on me being here to wipe up your puke forever.

JOHNNY: Nobody's asking you to.

IRENE: I'm tried of being the wife in your life, Johnny.
I'm not gonna hang around here and watch you wreck
yourself. . . . No thanks.

JOHNNY: I don't want to hear this.

IRENE: From now on, every time you get drunk, that's
one more step towards goodbye. . . . Not tomorrow or next
week, but soon, because it's not doing either of us any
good.

JOHNNY: Irene, it's too hot to get mad.

IRENE: Wish I was mad. Can't even cry about it anymore.

JOHNNY: Look, I'm going up to hospital next week.
There's a pill they got, it makes ya sick every time ya take
a drink.

IRENE: Johnny, you got to do it yourself.

JOHNNY: Okay, that's it for now. Okay? . . . You're right,
but it's the wrong time, okay? Okay?

IRENE goes into the house.

JOHNNY: *shouting after her*   Hey, Irene, is there any
more Coke in the fridge? Irene? . . . Fuck!

CECILE comes out to water her plants.

CECILE: Mes plantes. They get thirsty too.

JOHNNY: Eh?

CECILE: *holding up a plant*   See? . . . They're smiling.

*JOHNNY shrugs and gets up and turns off the TV. CECILE
goes back into her house.*

JOHNNY: Goddamn bums don't know how to win. . . .

THIBAULT: *to JOHNNY*   They're losing in French
too.

PAQUETTE: *watching TV*   Nos champions! L'ont
encore dans le cul, hostie.

JOHNNY: *to PAQUETTE*   So, Paquette, what do ya
think of the game? Eh?

THIBAULT: He don't speak the English no more.

JOHNNY: Oh, yeah?

THIBAULT: Oui, and me too. I don't speak the English
since last week. Maybe a few times, but that's all.

JOHNNY: Yeah, well, fuck the both of yas!

*He goes into his house and comes out with a Canadian flag
which he starts nailing up above his window.*

THIBAULT: *looking at JOHNNY's flag*   As-tu vu
ça, Paquette?

PAQUETTE: Tu t'as pompé là, hostie!

*PAQUETTE dashes into his house and comes out with a huge
Québec flag, which THIBAULT staples to the wall.*

PAQUETTE: Tabarnac! Tu m'en spotteras pas avec ça.
Thibault, viens m'aider, prends ton bord.

*THIBAULT goes over to help JOHNNY staples his flag above
the window. When JOHNNY turns around, he sees
PAQUETTE's huge Québec flag.*

JOHNNY: Fuck!

*He exits into his house. PAQUETTE and THIBAULT laugh.
They turn off their TV set and exit into PAQUETTE's house.*

The broadcast VOICE is heard again.

VOICE: Gaëtan Bolduc, the man for you . . . available and dynamic. . . . Gaëtan Bolduc, the man for you . . . available and dynamic. . . .

The sound fades away.

GAETAN BOLDUC enters and knocks on MURIEL's door.

MURIEL: *coming to the door*   Yeah, yeah. Hold your horses.   *She opens the door and sees BOLDUC.* Holy shit!

BOLDUC: Ah, bonjour. . . . Tu parles anglais? English?

MURIEL: Yeah.

BOLDUC: Ah. . . . I'm Gaëtan Bolduc, your Member of Parliament. We all know that something is wrong with Québec right now, eh?

MURIEL: You're goddamn right.

BOLDUC: Well, I would like to help fix it. . . . Bon. Here's my card with information. . . . Don't be afraid to call, eh?

MURIEL: Yeah, yeah.

BOLDUC: Don't forget me on the 6th.

MURIEL: Don't worry, I will.

She slams the door shut in his face. He goes up the stairs and knocks on JOHNNY's door.

IRENE: *inside the house*   Johnny. . . . There's someone at the door, Johnny. I'm in the tub.

JOHNNY: *inside the house*   Shit!

90

JOHNNY opens the door.

JOHNNY: You!

BOLDUC: Ah, bonjour.... Tu parles anglais? English?

JOHNNY: Yeah.

BOLDUC: Ah, I'm Gaëtan Bolduc, your Member of
Parliament....

JOHNNY: Oh, "Gaëtan Bolduc, the man for you...
available and dynamic." So, what can I do for you?

BOLDUC: No.... What can *I* do for you?

JOHNNY: You mean, what can I do *to* you?

BOLDUC: Bon. Here is my card with information. Don't
forget, a vote for Gaëtan Bolduc is a vote for me....
Bonjour.

JOHNNY: Hey! Wait a minute.... I'm not finished yet. I
only get to see you once every four years.

BOLDUC: Is there something you'd like to know?

JOHNNY: Yeah.... Houses are still burning down, there's
no jobs.... What happened to all them promises?

BOLDUC: It takes time.... We're working on it....

JOHNNY: Yeah? Eh, well, you got a lot of nerve walking
around here... and quit using Elvis music, okay? What's
the matter, you got no respect for the dead?

JOHNNY exits into his house.

IRENE: *from inside the house*   Johnny, what's that all
about?

JOHNNY: *from inside the house*   It's fuckface,
    Bolduc.

IRENE: *from inside the house*   Bolduc?

*BOLDUC knocks on PAQUETTE's door. DIANE answers the
door.*

DIANE: Oui?

BOLDUC: Etes-vous la femme de la maison?

DIANE: Moi? Jamais.... Paquette? Paquette, c'est
    Bolduc.

PAQUETTE: Quoi?

*THIBAULT sneaks out the window and goes downstairs where
he starts putting up more Bolduc posters. PAQUETTE comes
to the door.*

BOLDUC: Bonjour. Je suis Gaëtan Bolduc, votre député
    au parlement.

PAQUETTE: Salut, Gaëtan.

BOLDUC: Allô?

PAQUETTE: Tu me reconnais? Claude Paquette?...
    Ecole de Notre-Dame-des-Sept-Douleurs?

BOLDUC: Ah, oui.... Oui....

PAQUETTE: Claude Paquette....

BOLDUC: Claude Paquette?... Oui, c'est ça....

PAQUETTE: Tu sais que t'as l'air de pas t'arranger, mon
    Bolduc.

BOLDUC: Je travaille fort, tu sais. . . . On fait ce qu'on
    peut. . . .

PAQUETTE: Moi aussi. . . . J'travaille fort. Tu sais qu'j'ai
    jamais été sur le welfare. Moi, jamais. Les jeunes y se
    câlicent de ça, mais y faut que quelqu'un paye les taxes.
    Ces crisses de jeunes-là, y devraient toutes les câlicer dans
    l'armée. Comme ça, y travailleraient.

BOLDUC: Alors, tu vas voter pour moi, eh, Claude?

PAQUETTE: Fuck you! Tu me poigneras pas une
    deuxième fois!

*JOHNNY comes out and goes down the stairs. When he
reaches the bottom of the stairs, he turns around and throws
some eggs back at BOLDUC. They miss him and hit
PAQUETTE.*

PAQUETTE: Hey!

BOLDUC: C'est un joke, ça? Tu vas entendre parler de
    mes avocats, toi.

*BOLDUC comes down the stairs and exits hurriedly. JOHNNY
hands the eggs to THIBAULT to make it seem as if he had
thrown them. He exits after BOLDUC.*

PAQUETTE: Qu'est-ce que c'est ça? Qu'est-ce que c'est ça?

CECILE comes out. She looks at PAQUETTE.

CECILE: Claude, c'est quoi? Un oiseau?

THIBAULT starts coming up the stairs.

PAQUETTE: *to THIBAULT*   Thibault, est-ce que
    t'as qu'que chose sur la toiture?

THIBAULT: La toiture?

PAQUETTE: Oui. . . . La toiture.

THIBAULT looks up at the roof.

THIBAULT: Non.

PAQUETTE sees the eggs that JOHNNY has given to THIBAULT.

PAQUETTE: C'est quoi ça?

He takes the eggs from THIBAULT and starts throwing them at him. THIBAULT runs down the stairs.

THIBAULT: Hey! Hey!. . .

PAQUETTE: Ah, mon petit, tabarnac. . . .

JOHNNY enters and goes up the stairs to his balcony.

THIBAULT: C'est pas moi. C'est pas moi. . . .   *He points to JOHNNY.*   C'est lui. C'est lui.

JOHNNY stands on his balcony laughing.

PAQUETTE: C'est toi ça, eh? Big joke, eh? Big joke.

He throws an egg at JOHNNY.

JOHNNY: You watch yourself. . . . Okay?

JOHNNY crosses to PAQUETTE's balcony.

PAQUETTE: Hey, keep on your own side! Keep on your own side!

JOHNNY: You and Bolduc, eh? Ya suck!

PAQUETTE: Hey, c'est toi qui vote pour les Libérals, eh? Pas moi.

JOHNNY: Yeah, eh?

*They start shoving each other. IRENE comes out and she and
CECILE try to break up the fight.*

CECILE: Claude. . . .

IRENE: Johnny, stop it. . . .

IRENE starts hitting JOHNNY with a towel.

JOHNNY: What are ya hitting me for?

*IRENE exits into the house with JOHNNY in tow. DIANE
laughs at PAQUETTE from inside the house.*

PAQUETTE: La petite crisse, elle trouve ça drôle? Ça
    t'fait rire? Ça t'fait rire?

DIANE: *from inside the house*   Oui, je trouve ça
    drôle. . . . Lâche ça. . . . . Lâche ça. . . .

*PAQUETTE goes into the house, takes one of DIANE's records
and throws it out the window.*

PAQUETTE: Est-ce tu trouves ça drôle?

DIANE: *from inside the house*   Sors de ma
    chambre. . . . Va-t'en d'ici. . . .

TOM enters and knocks at MURIEL's door.

MURIEL: *coming to the door*   Yeah, yeah.   *She
    opens the door.*   You're back.

TOM: Yeah.

MURIEL: Well, you better wash up. . . . There's some
    food in the fridge.

TOM: Ma?

MURIEL: Yeah?

TOM: Uh...nothing....

He walks into the house.

*DIANE comes out of the house and sits in the rocking chair.
She is crying.*

JOHNNY comes out of his house and sits on the balcony.

CECILE comes out on her balcony.

CECILE: J'ai hâte qu'il fasse froid. Ton père peut pas
dormir quand il fait trop chaud. Ça le rend de mauvaise
humeur.

She checks her plants.

CECILE: C'est vrai. Il y a de la place ici. Je pense que je
vais déménager mes plantes sur le balcon d'en avant.

She sees that DIANE is crying.

CECILE: Diane....Diane, qu'est-ce qu'y a?

DIANE: Y a rien.

CECILE: Tu vas voir, ton père va être malheureux de ce
qu'il a fait, il va être gentil avec toi.

DIANE: Oui, mais j'suis pas un jouet, moi, maman.

CECILE: Diane....

DIANE: Laisse-moi tranquille....

CECILE goes back into her house.

JOHNNY: Irene? Hey, Irene?...

IRENE comes to the screen door.

IRENE: Yeah?

JOHNNY: Lend me a few bucks. I wanna go uptown. . . .
Yeah, yeah, I know. . . . Look, why don't you just tell me
to leave. Ya know, tell me to leave and it's all over.

IRENE: You're so weak.

JOHNNY: Just tell me it's over and I'm gone.

IRENE: I have to be strong for the both of us.

JOHNNY: It's so easy for you. You do this because of that.
You do that because of this. It's not that easy for me.

IRENE throws him five dollars.

IRENE: *yelling*   I hate you. . . . I hate you. . . .

She goes back into the house and slams the door.

JOHNNY: One more night, Irene. . . .

He exits.

*MURIEL comes out and throws a pair of boots in the garbage
can. TOM follows her out. He has nothing on his feet.*

TOM: Hey, Ma. . . . What are ya doing?

MURIEL: You're not wearing these. They stink.

TOM: What do ya mean?

MURIEL: They stink and I'm throwing them out.

TOM: Ma, it's the only pair of boots I've got.

MURIEL: You're not wearing them in the house . . . and just because your father is a bum, doesn't mean you have to be one too.

She goes back into the house. TOM takes the boots out of the garbage can and puts them back on.

TOM: She's nuts. I mean, she's clinical . . . .

DIANE: You? . . . You're back again?

TOM: Yeah. Did a circle . . . .

DIANE: Why did you come back here?

TOM: I had no choice . . . . Same old shit, eh?

DIANE: They drive me crazy, all these people . . . .

TOM: I know what you mean.

DIANE: They're not happy, so they want everybody else to be the same way.

TOM: Yeah . . . .

DIANE: Me? I want to get out . . . . But how? Where do you go?

TOM: Not to Ormstown, I'll tell ya that . . . . Bunch of farmers . . . .

DIANE: You don't like New York City?

TOM: Never got there . . . . Wouldn't let me cross the border . . . . No money.

DIANE: You need money, eh?

TOM: Yeah.

DIANE: Always the same thing. . . .

TOM: Yeah. They don't make it easy for ya.

DIANE: They?. . .Oui. . .they.

TOM: You, uh. . .get my letter?

DIANE: Oui.

TOM: So. . . .What do ya think?

DIANE: Why do you worry about what I think?

TOM: I don't know. . . .

DIANE: The letter was. . .okay.

TOM: Oh yeah? I meant what I said, ya know?. . .In the letter.

DIANE: I'm not beautiful.

TOM: I don't know. . . .Girls that never blink turn me on.

DIANE: That's too bad for you.

TOM: Hey, uh. . . .I'm gonna look for work here and when I got some money, maybe I'll try New York again.

DIANE: What for? It's the same thing everywhere.

TOM: Hey, uh. . .you're in a good mood, eh?

PAQUETTE comes out carrying some pop bottles down the stairs.

PAQUETTE: Hey, Diane. Je m'en vas au magasin. As-tu besoin de qu'que chose?

DIANE: Je veux rien qui vient de toi.

PAQUETTE: Tu pourrais au moins être polie, câlice, apart de ça. J't'ai pas dit que j'voulais pas que tu t'tiennes avec les têtes carrées.

DIANE: You don't tell me what to do.

PAQUETTE: Crisse, parle-moi en français, par exemple.

DIANE: Fuck you!

PAQUETTE: *to TOM*   Et toi-là. Keep on your own side.

He exits.

TOM: Good to be home again. . . .

DIANE: Nobody tells me what to do. . . . Nobody.

TOM: All those French guys over thirty. . . . Grease!

DIANE: Et toi, tête carrée. What do you look like, eh?

TOM: Don't know. . . . Have to wear a box for a hat, I guess.

DIANE: That's right. . . . Aw, it's so hot!

TOM: You, uh, want to take a walk?. . . No, eh?

DIANE: A walk?

TOM: Yeah, a walk.

DIANE: Where?

TOM: I don't know. . . the Boardwalk? I always walk there.

DIANE: Okay.

TOM: Uh . . . which way?

DIANE: I don't care.

TOM: This way . . . .

They begin to exit.

MURIEL comes out of the house.

MURIEL: Tom?

TOM: Yeah?

MURIEL: Just look at you. . . . You're a mess!

TOM: We're going for a walk.

MURIEL: Tom, come here. . . . I want to speak to you. . . .

TOM: What?

MURIEL: Do you think this is fair to me?

TOM: What?

MURIEL: All of this? . . .

TOM: I guess not.

MURIEL: You guess not?

TOM: Look, I had nothing to do with this. I was just
born here, that's all.

MURIEL: Listen, don't think you can start in all over,
hanging around here daydreaming, 'cause I won't have it.
Either you get a job or you get out. It's one or the
other . . . .

TOM: Job! Job! Job! I'm gonna get a job!

MURIEL: I've heard that one before.

TOM: This time, I'm gonna look.

MURIEL: Sure. . . and then, you'll move out with your first cheque.

TOM: Ma?

MURIEL: Don't you "Ma" me.

TOM: Ma? I don't wanna fight with ya, Ma.

MURIEL: So, don't fight. . . .

MURIEL exits into her house.

TOM: Home, sweet home. . . .

He bangs a garbage can and exits down the lane with DIANE.

Blackout.

Scene Three

The sound of sawing is heard offstage. JOHNNY is in the shed working. CLAUDE enters carrying his lunch bucket. He is coming home from work early. CECILE is watering her plants on the balcony.

CECILE: Claude, t'es de bonne heure. Qu'est-ce qui arrive? Es-tu malade?

PAQUETTE: Non, je ne suis pas malade.

CECILE: Qu'est-ce qu'y a qui va pas?

PAQUETTE: J'ai perdu ma job. Je suis revenu à pied.

CECILE: Veux-tu une chaise, Claude?

PAQUETTE: Pas une crisse d'avertissement. Je suis allé voir le boss en haut. Il a dit que ça lui faisait ben de la peine, mais il pouvait rien faire. Là, je suis allé voir le gars de l'union. Tu sais ce qu'il m'a dit, le gars de l'union, eh? "There's nothing we can do. The company is stopping their operation in Montréal. They're going to relocate it in Taiwan."... Taïwan!

CECILE: Taïwan? C'est au Vermont, ça?

PAQUETTE: Treize ans de ma vie.... Treize ans de ma câlice de vie....

CECILE: Quatorze, Claude. Je me souviens. Quand t'as eu ta job, c'était en octobre.

PAQUETTE: J'ai quarante-deux ans, tabarnac. J'peux pas recommencer à zéro. Qu'est-ce que j'vas faire?

CECILE: Tu l'aimais pas ta job de toute façon.

PAQUETTE: J'sais que je l'aimais pas, mais y faut ben manger.

CECILE: Oui.

PAQUETTE: Les crisses y sont ben toutes pareils. Les tabarnacs. Y s'servent de toi pis quand y'ont pu besoin de toi, y te câlicent dehors comme un vieux torchon sale. Pis, fuck you! Mange d'la merde. Pis si tu meures, c'est encore mieux. Y'ont pu de welfare à payer.

CECILE: Welfare? Mais on a jamais été sur le welfare, Claude.

PAQUETTE: Cécile, c'est pas de ma faute. C'est pas de ma faute.

CECILE: Je sais que je dis des choses stupides, mais je sais pas quoi dire.

The broadcast VOICE is heard.

VOICE: Don't forget tomorrow. Voting day. . . . Re-elect Gaëtan Bolduc, the man for you. . . available and dynamic. . . .

The sound fades away.

DIANE and TOM enter together.

DIANE: "Apocalypse Now?" C'est quoi, "Apocalypse Now?"

TOM: It's a film about that war there in the States.

DIANE: What war?

TOM: Uh. . .China. . . .Somewhere over there. . . . Wanna go? Tonight?

DIANE: Okay. . . .Salut. . . .

She goes up the stairs.

TOM: See ya. . . .

He goes into his house.

DIANE: *at the top of the stairs* Allô, Maman. Ça va?

PAQUETTE: Diane, tu peux oublier ton école.

DIANE: Qu'est-ce qu'y lui prend lui?

CECILE: Ton père a perdu sa job

DIANE: Sa job?

CECILE: Oui, Diane.

DIANE: Bon. Y a pas d'quoi se plaindre.

CECILE: Ah, Diane.

DIANE: C'est bien mieux de même. Comme ça, on
l'entendra plus chicaner. Cette job-là, nous a toutes
rendus fous. C'est vrai.

CECILE: Elle est jeune, Claude.

PAQUETTE: Laisse-la faire.

DIANE: Je vais m'en trouver une job, moi. Inquiète-toi
pas. C'est facile. Ils ont toujours besoin de waitress cute.
Puis moi, je suis cute. Je vais en parler avec Irene, okay?

PAQUETTE: Moi, il faut que je fasse quelque chose.

DIANE: Va quelque part avec Cécile. Vous êtes libres, là.
C'est le temps ou jamais. Oubliez ça pour un bout de
temps.

PAQUETTE: Oh, non.

CECILE: Mais où est-ce qu'on irait?

PAQUETTE: Diane, tu te souviens quand tu étais petite,
petite de même, on montait en haut sur la montagne, eh?
On regardait les beaux arbres, les beaux oiseaux. C'était
beau, hein? Diane, j'ai toujours voulu ce qu'il y avait de
mieux pour toi. Je suis fatigué. Je ne sais plus quoi dire.

CECILE: Viens t'allonger, Claude. Viens t'allonger.

CECILE helps CLAUDE to the door.

DIANE: Papa.

They exit into the house. DIANE sits on a chair on the balcony.

MURIEL and IRENE enter.

IRENE: So, what did they say this time?

MURIEL: Ah, you know doctors. . . . They just try to scare ya. . . .

IRENE: Hey, you're going to be okay.

MURIEL: Nope. They said it was serious.

IRENE: Yeah? How serious?

MURIEL: I'm gonna have an operation.

IRENE: Oh no, Muriel.

MURIEL: Yeah. . . . On the stomach. Ulcers.

IRENE: Oh no.

MURIEL: Aw, now that I know what they're gonna do, I'm not worried about it. It's just thinking about it that drives ya nuts.

IRENE: Ulcers. . . . Hey, so I was right, eh?

MURIEL: Yeah. Now, I'm gonna have to drink lots of milk. . . . Yuk!

IRENE: Does Tom know?

MURIEL: Yeah, he seems worried about it.

IRENE: Well, of course. . . .

MURIEL: Ya know what those bastard doctors told me? Told me, I had to stop being so nervous. . . . Yeah, there's this fat pig making $80,000.00 a year, living in Côte Saint-Luc, telling me not to be a nervous wreck. . . . Well, I got so mad, I tell ya. . . . I got so mad, I couldn't talk.

IRENE: I can't blame ya.

MURIEL: It makes ya wanna kill yourself just out of spite.

IRENE: Ya oughta go to the clinic in the Pointe. The doctors there treat ya like a human being.

MURIEL: I dunno. . . . I heard they're all Commies or something.

IRENE: So what?

MURIEL: Yeah, well, guess they couldn't be any worse. . . . Oh, Irene, wait. . . . I wanna show ya something.

MURIEL takes a small box out of her purse and opens it.

MURIEL: Look.

IRENE: A brooch. . . . That's beautiful.

MURIEL: Tom bought it for me with his first pay.

IRENE: It's beautiful.

MURIEL: Yeah. . . . Stupid kid. Now, he doesn't have enough money for car fare.

JOHNNY enters from the shed carrying some lumber and some tools. He has built a new step for the stairs.

IRENE: Does he like his new job?

MURIEL: Well, he's lasted a month. That's some kind of
       record.

She sees JOHNNY and the step.

MURIEL: Holy shit! Hey, watch your thumbs!

JOHNNY glares at her.

MURIEL: Just a joke. . . .

She goes into her house.

JOHNNY: Irene, gimme a hand with this. . . . Yeah, I
       know, officially, we ain't talking, but I need a hand. . . .

IRENE: I don't believe it.

She goes over to help JOHNNY put the new step in place.

JOHNNY: So, what's new? . . . How are ya?

IRENE: I don't know. . . . Haven't been talking to myself
       lately.

JOHNNY: I've been off the sauce for a week now, right?

IRENE: Yeah.

JOHNNY: Yeah. . . .

IRENE: You want a medal or what?

JOHNNY: Irene. . . . It's not easy, okay?

IRENE: Try being a woman for a while. . . .

DIANE: *from upstairs*   Oui, that's right.

JOHNNY takes IRENE over to one side.

JOHNNY: Irene, all that crap about you being strong for the both of us. . . .

IRENE: It's not crap.

JOHNNY: Yeah, okay. . . .It's true, but I didn't make up the rules of the game, okay? I mean, it wasn't me.

IRENE: It wasn't me.

JOHNNY: I'm sorry, Irene. You know that?. . .I'm sorry.

IRENE: I was worried. . . .

JOHNNY: About what?

IRENE: I've never seen you that bad before. . . .

JOHNNY: Hey, I don't melt in the rain. . . .I don't get diarrhea in the snow. I'm a survivor.

IRENE: Yeah. . . .

They embrace.

IRENE: So, what are ya gonna do?

JOHNNY: Maybe I can get back into music.

IRENE: You've been miserable ever since ya quit playing. . . .

JOHNNY: You're the one who nagged me to quit.

IRENE: All I wanted you to do was stop drinking and screwing around so much. . . .Music had nothing to do with it.

JOHNNY: What do you know about the nightlife, Irene?

IRENE: Yeah, well. . . . Anyhow, no matter what happens, we'll always be friends, eh?

JOHNNY: Is that a threat?

IRENE: Yeah.

TOM comes out with his guitar and starts to play a song.

IRENE: Hi, Tommy.

IRENE goes up the stairs and into the house. JOHNNY comes over to talk to TOM.

JOHNNY: So, how's the new job?

TOM: Aw, Troy Laundry. . . . What can I say? Some guys been there twenty years and I'm there twenty days and already going nuts.

JOHNNY: Bad news, eh?

TOM: Hey. Can't talk to anybody. . . . They're all deaf from the noise.

JOHNNY: They probably got nothing to say anyhow.

TOM: Ya don't get a watch when ya retire, ya get a hearing aid.

CECILE comes out on her balcony to speak to DIANE.

CECILE: Tu sais, Diane, j'ai vu ton père pleurer juste une fois. C'est quand t'étais petite puis bien malade.

DIANE: Je ne me souviens pas de ça.

CECILE: Ça fait longtemps. On restait sur la rue Joseph.

TOM plays a tune on his guitar.

TOM: *to DIANE*   Hi, Diane....You like that?...

DIANE: No....Know any disco?

TOM: Disco!...Disco duck....I don't got the right buttons on this thing.

MURIEL: *from inside the house*   Tommy?

TOM: Yeah?

MURIEL: I'm gonna need a hand in here....I'm moving out your old man's junk into the shed.

TOM: You're moving it out?

MURIEL: Yeah....He's never here and we can use the room.

TOM: Okay.

He goes in to help her move the things out to the shed.

IRENE comes out of her house and goes down the stairs.

IRENE: All the trouble that step caused us over the last year and look at that, it's fixed.

JOHNNY: Yeah, I'm gonna send Giboux the bill.

DIANE: *to IRENE*   Irene, is there any jobs at your place?

IRENE: What?

DIANE: I have to find work. My father, he lost his job.

IRENE: He lost his job?

CECILE: Yes. The company is going to Taiwan, but they don't want to take Claude.

IRENE: The bastards.

JOHNNY: He got the axe, eh?

IRENE: How is he?

DIANE: Not so good. . . . Maybe you can talk to him,
    Irene.

IRENE: Be better if you talk to him, Johnny.

JOHNNY: What the fuck am I gonna say? He don't even
    want to speak my language.

IRENE: *shouting to MURIEL*   Hey, Muriel. Paquette
    lost his job.

MURIEL comes out of her house.

MURIEL: What? Another one for your Unemployment
    Committee.   *To CECILE.*   Sorry, madame. I
    really am.

IRENE: We can get him out on our next demonstration.

JOHNNY: Another one?

IRENE: We're gonna march in front of the U.I.C.
    building. Let them know we don't like the forty percent
    unemployment down here.

JOHNNY: Demonstration in the Pointe? That's not news.

MURIEL: We should do it in Westmount. That's where
    all the money is. Go up there and sit on their goddamn
    front lawns.

DIANE: Oui. Go right up there and let them know what
    we look like.

TOM: Yeah.

CECILE: It's very nice up in Westmount. . . . It's very nice.

JOHNNY: Yeah, you can take Thibault and leave him up there. . . . Boom! Into the woodwork. . . . Westmount's infested. . . . Thousands of little Thibault's running around. . . . Boom! Another Pointe Saint-Charles!

MURIEL: Thibault. . . . Our secret weapon.

TOM: So secret, he don't even know.

IRENE: Johnny, talk to Paquette. . . .

JOHNNY: You talk to him. . . .

IRENE: Johnny?

JOHNNY: Look, it's the principle of the thing. . . .

IRENE: Principle of what?

JOHNNY: Well, he started it, right?

IRENE: Started what?

DIANE: Maudit crisse, Johnny!

JOHNNY: Alright. Ya want me to be the nice guy. . . . Why do I always got to be the nice guy?

He goes up the stairs and knocks on PAQUETTE's door.

JOHNNY: Hey, Porky. . . . Peace in the valley, okay?

PAQUETTE: *from inside his house*   Quoi?

JOHNNY: Let's kiss and make up.

PAQUETTE: Quoi?

IRENE: Tell him you're sorry he lost his job.

JOHNNY: Look, I'm sorry you lost your job. . . .

IRENE: Tell him in French.

JOHNNY: I don't know how.

IRENE: Try. . . .J'ai de la peine. . . .

JOHNNY: J'ai de la peine. . . .

IRENE: J'ai de la peine que tu as perdu. . .que tu as
perdu. . . .

JOHNNY: J'ai de la peine que tu as perdu. . . .

IRENE: Ta job.

JOHNNY: Ta fuckin' job. . . .He's not talking.

IRENE: He's upset.

JOHNNY: Diane, how do you say, "Together, we can fuck
Bolduc?

DIANE: "Ensemble on peut fourrer Bolduc."

JOHNNY: Hey, Paquette. . . ."Ensemble. . . ."

PAQUETTE: *at his screen door*   Hey, you go away
with the bullshit, okay? Take it somewhere else. . . .It's
just another Pepsi who loses his job. T'es content. . . .
Alors, viens pas m'écoeurer avec ça.

He slams the door shut.

JOHNNY: Irene!

He goes into his house and slams his door shut.

IRENE: Oh boy!

*She goes up the stairs to PAQUETTE's door and knocks on it.
There is no answer.*

MURIEL: Talking's easy, Irene, but try to get people
     together. . . . Ppphht?

IRENE: What does it take to move you guys?. . . We gotta
     help ourselves. That's easy to understand, isn't it?

DIANE: They don't want to understand. . . . It's easier to
     eat shit.

IRENE: I don't know why I bother.

MURIEL: Ah, we can still do the demonstration without
     them.

CECILE: We need the government to help us.

MURIEL: What are you talking about? Bolduc *is* the
     government!

IRENE: Well. . . . I'm tired. . . .

*THIBAULT enters on his bike. He has a case of beer for
PAQUETTE.*

THIBAULT: Chez Momo's is here.

TOM: Hey, Thibault. How's the girls?

THIBAULT: Oh boy, don't talk to me about that. . . .
     Trouble all the time. . . .

He goes up the stairs and discovers the new step.

THIBAULT: Hey!

He dances on the new step.

THIBAULT: Où est Paquette?

He puts the case of beer down on the balcony.

CECILE: Claude est pas bien aujourd'hui. Il a perdu sa job.

THIBAULT: Il a perdu sa job? Aw, everybody's got trouble now, eh? Me, last week, I got hit by a Cadillac.

MURIEL: By a what?

THIBAULT: A Cadillac, oui.... Big car, eh?... So, I phone the boss and he says, "How's the bike?" "How's the bike?" hostie.... Hey, me, I know the boss. Sometimes he talks nice, but he's still the boss, eh?

MURIEL: Aw, bosses.... They're all the same, Thibault.

THIBAULT: Sure, I know that.... Maybe I'm crazy, but I'm not stupid, eh?

MURIEL: They do what they want, the bastards. They always do what they want.

She starts ripping down Bolduc posters.

THIBAULT: Hey. Bolduc won't like that....

MURIEL: Ppphht on Bolduc.

THIBAULT: Okay.... He won't like that, that's all.

DIANE: Irene, do you smell something?

IRENE: Yeah....

TOM: Probably someone burning garbage.

MURIEL: Do you see any smoke?

IRENE: Yeah, but I don't know where it's coming from.

CECILE: C'est un feu.

THIBAULT: Un feu? Où ça un feu?

IRENE: *to JOHNNY, inside the house*   Johnny, go down the lane and take a look.

JOHNNY comes out of his house.

JOHNNY: Why do I always have to do everything around here?

He dashes off down the lane, followed by TOM and DIANE. They all yell, "Fire!" JOHNNY comes running back on.

JOHNNY: Irene, call the cops! It's a big one! Just a few houses down. . . .

He runs back down the lane.

CECILE: Claude? Claude, y a un feu!

IRENE: I can't get the cops. The lines are busy. . . .

PAQUETTE comes running out of his house.

CECILE: Claude, dis à Diane de ne pas aller trop proche. . . .

He exits down the lane.

IRENE: It's a big one.

CECILE: Oh, yes. . .a big one. . . .

MURIEL: Those old houses go up like matchsticks. . . .

PAQUETTE: *yelling offstage*   Ça s'étend aux sheds d'à côté!

CECILE: Mon Dieu!

MURIEL: What did he say?

IRENE: It's spreading. . . .

MURIEL: Where the hell are the firemen?

IRENE: If this were Westmount, there wouldn't be a fire.

IRENE: Yeah, right. . . .

PAQUETTE comes running back on.

PAQUETTE: Ça continue à s'étendre!

MURIEL: What's he saying?

PAQUETTE: Cécile, on va sortir les meubles!

*JOHNNY comes running back on, followed by TOM and
DIANE.*

JOHNNY: Hey, Irene, start moving our stuff out!

*There is general running around and shouting. THIBAULT
gets in everyone's way. JOHNNY and PAQUETTE carry down
their TV sets and their beer first. CECILE carries down her
plants.*

MURIEL: Tom, move your ass!

TOM: Aw, we're insured anyhow. . . .

MURIEL: Move it!

PAQUETTE: *to CECILE*   C'est pas le temps toi et pis
     tes hostie de plantes.

MURIEL: Thibault, get your bike out of the way!

THIBAULT: Hey, don't touch my bike!

MURIEL: Then, get it out of the way!

THIBAULT: Eh, Madame Paquette, y a un gros feu
    là-bas! Hey, good thing we fix that step, eh?

JOHNNY: *to PAQUETTE*   Keep your shit on that
    side. . . .

PAQUETTE: Va donc chier, câlice!

*JOHNNY and PAQUETTE collide at the top of the stairs.
They start pushing and shoving each other to see who will go
down the stairs first.*

PAQUETTE: Ote-toi de là, hostie!

JOHNNY: Get out of my way!

IRENE, CECILE and DIANE rush in to break up the fight.

IRENE: Don't be so stupid. . . . Now, get out of the
    way. . . both of you. Come, you guys. . . . Hey, Muriel,
    Tom. . . . We'll do a relay. . . . We'll move them out
    upstairs, then we'll do you.

MURIEL: Why upstairs first?

IRENE: Muriel, come on!

*The relay begins. They all start passing stuff down. It comes at
them through the windows and through the doors.
PAQUETTE calls JOHNNY over to get him to give him a hand
with the sofa.*

PAQUETTE: Lève-toi. . . . Lève-le. . . .

JOHNNY: Irene, he's speaking French!

IRENE: Lift it!

PAQUETTE: Tourne-le. . . . Tourne-le. . . .

JOHNNY: Yeah, yeah. . . tour-ney. . . .

PAQUETTE: A droite. . . .

IRENE: To the right.

PAQUETTE: Laisse-le slyer sur la rampe. . . . La rampe. . . .

JOHNNY: What???

IRENE: Slide it down the banister!

They slide the sofa down the banister. JOHNNY hurts himself when he and PAQUETTE put the sofa down at the foot of the stairs.

PAQUETTE: Okay, allez, Johnny. . . . We go move ton sofa. . . .

He helps JOHNNY up the stairs.

When they get halfway up the stairs, a huge crashing noise is heard.

TOM: There goes the roof!

CECILE: Mon Dieu!

IRENE: Here it comes. . . .

MURIEL: Christ, we're next!

The broadcast VOICE is heard once again.

VOICE: Citizens of Pointe Saint-Charles, we live in a time when we need a strong government, a just government, one that is not afraid to deal harshly with disrupters, sabotage, corruptions and criminals. Remember a vote for Gaëtan Bolduc is a vote for security, for justice, for law and order. . . . and for the future. Le futur. . . .

JOHNNY, IRENE, MURIEL AND TOM: *turning to the audience* What are we going to do?

PAQUETTE, CECILE, DIANE AND THIBAULT: *turning to the audience* Qu'est-ce qu'on va faire?

Blackout.